Baptism

THE BELIEVER'S WEDDING CEREMONY

F. LAGARD SMITH

GOSPEL
ADVOCATE
PUBLISHERS
BOOKS · MAGAZINES · CURRICULUM
P.O. BOX 150
NASHVILLE, TN 37202

Published by Gospel Advocate Company
P.O. Box 150, Nashville, TN 37202

ISBN 0-89225-422-X

Acknowledgments

In an attempt to join discussion with all fellowships throughout the Christian community, I have submitted my manuscript in various draft stages to several persons whose view are representative of those considered in the book. Each one has been graciously accommodative in furthering my attempt to present the issues common to us all. My deepest gratitude is extended to Tony Coffey, Dublin, Ireland; Brady Smith, Lausanne, Switzerland; Rubel Shelley, Nashville, Tennessee; Bob Owen and Colly G. Caldwell, Temple terrace, Florida; Jonathan Vick and Dan Anders, Malibu, California; and Bill Jensen, Eugene, Oregon—who have carefully monitored my analysis, arguments, and attitude.

My appreciation also goes to Craig Blomberg of the Denver Seminary; William J. Richardson of Emmanuel School of Religion; Marshall Hayden of Worthington Christian Church; and William Baker of St. Louis Christian College, each of whom provided an excellent scholarly critique of my work and suggested important changes.

I am particularly grateful to Willy and Betty Grunder of the English Church in Davos, Switzerland; Richard Bewes and Ian Bentley of All Souls Church, London; Robert F. Cochran, Sr. of the Bon Air Baptist Church, Virginia; John Sheridan of Our Lady of Malibu; Michael Roebert of St. John Seminary, Camarillo; and Aidan Kavanagh of Yale Divinity School—who allowed me to invade their busy schedules to ask questions and to present for their response a baptismal doctrine foreign to their own. While none of these would agree with all the conclusions I have presented, I greatly appreciate that we have been able to work together in a spirit of love and mutual respect to search out God's will regarding baptism.

Special thanks go to Jim Woodroof, Shirley Roper, and Richardson R. Lynn, who have carefully crafted my words into a more readable presentation and have provided substantive suggestions to enrich the book's content.

Dedication

Dedicated to the memory of
Valentine I. Stirman and Rollin R. Stirman,

pioneer preachers
through whom I have received a rich spiritual heritage.

Table of Contents

CHAPTER 1

Meaning From Murky Waters

"No athlete is admitted to the contest of virtue, unless he has first been washed of all stains of sins and consecrated with the gift of heavenly grace."

St. Ambrose

At fourteen I was the last holdout among the teenagers in our little congregation. It wasn't that I questioned the need to be baptized, but I wanted to do it only when I was sure I was ready. There were constant reminders that I was not yet fully accepted into the fellowship of believers. When the bread and "fruit of the vine" were passed among the worshipers during our weekly observance of Communion, I passed them along to the next person without partaking, as if shouting out an admission that I was not yet a Christian. And when young men were being chosen to pass the Communion, of course, I was never asked. There was also subtle pressure from certain members of the congregation who wondered why the preacher's son was the last of the young people in his age group to "respond to the invitation." Fortunately, neither my mother nor my father said a word, or even hinted that I was past the time of making the big decision. But my older sisters had not let it escape their attention. A well-meaning comment here and there, or a story told within my hearing about someone my age who had been killed in an accident before he was baptized, showed their fear of what could happen to me if I continued to drag my feet. And whenever the subject arose at church among my friends—all of whom had been baptized at various ages from nine to thirteen—they exhibited what I felt to be a self-righteous air about their now-confirmed status as Christians.

I returned the smugness in my own mind, believing that they had been baptized solely out of a fear of going to hell, or because they wanted to please their parents, or because some visiting preacher had successfully played on their immature emotions. Some of them had been baptized in pairs or groups, like teaming up to undergo a fraternity initiation. Whatever else was going through my mind in those awkward teenage years, I resolved that I would not be baptized just because it was expected of me.

In our fellowship, the preacher extended an invitation to the unsaved and wayward at the conclusion of every sermon, and the congregation would stand together to sing. I know I was not alone in dreading "invitation" songs. Many an impenitent or unbaptized soul has endured the agony of waiting out those three or four seemingly endless verses calling the sinner home.

I just *knew* all eyes were on me. "LaGard's still not budging," I imagined someone saying. "Wouldn't you think his father would have a talk with him?" I assumed another might be thinking. Sometimes I think I might have been baptized much earlier had it not been for all the good souls who, to my mind, at least, were wagging their all-too-righteous heads. And yet there were also times I wanted to be baptized just to get it over with— just to be relieved of all the pressure.

When it finally happened, I was as surprised as anyone. I hadn't plotted or planned it. No one said a word or led the way down the aisle. It just happened. That Sunday morning, we had a visiting preacher in the pulpit. I can't even recall what his sermon was about. But when the first words of the invitation song were sung, I moved quickly down the aisle to the front of the auditorium where my father was waiting to receive me.

Before I could reflect on it further, I made my public confession of faith in Jesus Christ, changed into starchy white baptismal garb, and stepped down into the cold, murky, almost slimy water typical of seldom-used baptistries.

With the now-disturbed water lapping around me, it was as if I were standing in the river that flowed through the peaceful valley in the other-worldly painting on the wall above me. Anyone growing up in churches with landscape murals painted above the baptistries will know that scene. They all seem to have been painted by the same artist.

As my father put one arm around my back and raised the other into the air heavenward, I heard him say the words I had heard on so many other occasions. This time they had special meaning to me. "Upon your confession of faith in Jesus Christ, and in obedience to His command to teach and baptize the nations, I now baptize you for the forgiveness of your sins, in the name of the Father, and of the Son, and of the Holy Spirit. Amen." With that, I was quickly plunged beneath the water and brought back to the surface—thrilled, refreshed, and fully committed.

Commitment to an Act, Commitment to a Life

I now know that, at the age of fourteen, I had barely become acquainted with sin—*real* sin. That would come years later, when youthful commitment would be torn to shreds by the savage onslaught of a sinful world; when memories of that cold, murky baptistry and those majestic words would have all but faded.

What, then, was the value of my baptism experience? Did it keep me from future sin? Of course not. Did it dramatically transform my life-style? Not really. To this day I wrestle with sin, struggle with relationships, and fight my carnal nature. But somehow, in that optimistic act of baptism, I was telling myself and the whole world that I was *committed* to wrestle, *committed* to struggle, and *committed* to fight for what I knew to be good and right. The issue was not a lifetime of winning or losing. I knew even then that always winning was a hopeless human goal. Baptism meant commitment to a purpose and to a new relationship with God. And it still does.

It is easy to convince oneself that spiritual life begins with an identifiable conversion experience. For many, that may be true. If one's life was filled with blatant acts of immorality, the newness of Christ living within must be like a change in personality. At times, I envy such people. They seem to appreciate fully their salvation. They are usually vocal in their praise to God and eager to share the good news about Jesus Christ. Having been so close to spiritual death, how they now love the Great Physician!

Ironically, they may envy those of us who were raised in Christian families, without understanding that, in at least one important respect, this can be as much a curse as a blessing. The child who is brought up by faithful Christian parents to be a believer in Jesus Christ and to live a substantially righteous life may be cheated out of a dramatic, lifestyle-changing conversion experience. For that person, baptism can be more a formality than a transformation. More a rational decision than an emotional response to a previously unknown love.

By the time I was baptized, I had been a believer in Jesus Christ for many years. My earliest notions about

Jesus came from flannel board and sandbox lessons in Sunday school, as well as from Bible stories read to me by my mother. By the age of fourteen, I was a good student of the Bible and had memorized many more verses than I know now. I had no doubt that I would live my entire life according to Jesus' teaching because I already had a personal relationship with Jesus Christ. Without making any public confession to that effect, I had already come to believe in Him as the one who would be Lord and Savior of my life. But from all I had been taught, I was not yet a Christian. I had not been baptized.

Blurred Images of Baptism

Not until years later would I analyze in greater depth the teaching of those in my fellowship on the subject of baptism. In our church, there seemed to be three basic doctrinal approaches.

The first approach was best summarized in the expression most often used when referring to someone who had just been baptized: "Have you heard the good news? John finally *obeyed the gospel*." Being baptized and "obeying the gospel" were interchangeable concepts. This approach suggested that baptism was the focus of one's obedience to Christ's teaching. Not the beginning of one's obedience, but the culmination of it.

In fairness, there was abundant teaching from the pulpit in our fellowship that baptism, though highly significant, is only one demonstrable way in which we obey the gospel of Christ. The obedient daily life of the Christian was also stressed. Yet, to the extent that the implication remained—that baptism was the focus of one's obedience—there lay the danger that one could believe his salvation was complete at that point, regardless of how he lived his life thereafter.

The second approach was a subtle syllogism, never stated in quite this fashion, but frequently close:

11

> Only those who are in Christ's church will go to Heaven.
>
> In order to be a member of Christ's church, you must be baptized.
>
> Therefore, if you want to go to Heaven, you must be baptized into the church.

Again, in fairness, there was abundant teaching urging the hearer to be baptized into Christ; to share in His death, burial, and resurrection; and to put on the new man—to be born again of the water and the Spirit.

But untold numbers of hearers may never have got past the natural implication of the basic syllogism—that we are baptized into Christ's *church* rather than into *Christ himself.* Saying that those who are baptized into Christ also comprise His church—the body of Christ—is not the same as calling on people to be baptized *into the church.* Because so many people see "the church" as some local group of believers who meet together from week to week in the same house of worship, it is easy for the unsuspecting to confuse the universal, spiritual body of Christ with a local church or some identifiable denomination.

There is great danger that this view of baptism will lead a person to regard himself more as a "member of the church" than as simply a new Christian. What one is baptized into has a way of becoming that to which he owes his highest allegiance. What one is baptized into becomes that to which he will attribute his salvation.

And there is danger, too, in suggesting that one's salvation is in some way corporate rather than personal— that one finds his way to God through a church rather than through a personal faith in Jesus. Even in the natural world, one is born as an individual, and only coincidentally happens to be part of a family. No one is born in order to become part of a particular family.

The third approach saw baptism as part of a rather stiff, almost mathematical formula whereby, in order to become a Christian, one had to (1) hear, (2) believe, (3) repent, (4) confess, and (5) be baptized. In effect, salvation was given the numerical equivalent of 5, and each step the equivalent of 1. When each step had been accomplished, the sum total gave the correct result for salvation. Using this approach, baptism became the pinkie in a five-finger outline.

To say that there is a Biblical pattern for conversion in which belief, repentance, confession, and baptism all play dynamic parts is crucially different from parroting a rigid formula requiring certain "steps to salvation." My first clue that something was wrong with our particular formula was the apparent need to include step #1—hearing—as a requirement for salvation. While hearing the Word of God is a prerequisite for faith and for the acts of faith that follow, "hearing" hardly qualifies as a spiritual requirement on a check-off list for salvation.

The danger of replacing a dynamic heartfelt decision with a legalistic formula—be it be the one I have outlined or the widley used Four Spiritual Laws or any other—ought to be apparent. Granted, there may be benefits to be gained by the simple, easily-recognizable packaging of spiritual truth. But there is great risk that any such formula will become a sectarian Shibboleth, achieving more sectarian exclusivity than the conversion results it is intended to produce. Baptism in particular must never be reduced to anything like a "step" or a "law" as an end in itself.

Outward Sign of Inward Grace?

If these views of baptism seem skewed and potentially dangerous, there are other approaches—held far more widely throughout the Christian community—that suffer equally in their doctrinal or practical implications. Take, for example, the view that baptism is an outward sign of an inward grace—that if baptism is essential, it is so because it is commanded, and not because it has any substantive role in one's salvation.

Perhaps you grew up in a fellowship that took this or some similar view of baptism. If so, you will recognize that, according to this view of baptism, the believer becomes a Christian through faith and the acceptance of Christ as Lord of his life. Only then, subsequent to one's initial salvation, is one expected to be baptized as an act of obedience. Thus viewed, baptism is symbolic of a relationship that *already exists* rather than being part of the conversion process that *initiates* the relationship.

Behind this view of baptism is a legitimate fear that any other view of baptism makes it a required "work" on the part of the believer, contrary to the clear teaching of Scripture that salvation is by grace, not by the believer's own efforts. Yet because this view suggests to the believer that baptism has no intrinsic role in the process of salvation, there is great danger of baptism's losing its dynamic spiritual significance, and becoming only a legal requirement.

To be fair, those who hold this view would insist that anyone who refuses to obey the Lord's command to be baptized lacks true commitment, and raises a serious question regarding his salvation. But again, failing to see baptism as an integral part of salvation reduces it to mere ceremony and formality—to make it more an after-the-fact initiation into a church than an act of covenant with God.

It is a common notion that the real purpose of baptism is to become a member of some church, or even to get one's name on the membership roll of some local congregation. One sometimes hears, for example, "I was baptized Baptist," or "I was baptized Methodist." While I know of no fellowship that actually teaches this sectarian view, it is not surprising that it would be associated with the view that one is saved at the point of faith, and baptized later for some reason apart from salvation.

14

Infant Baptism?

To this point, the various views of baptism that have been presented have all presupposed adult participation in the act. But the only baptism that most people have experienced was one that took place when they were infants. Perhaps that is your own baptismal experience. Without discussing now the doctrinal concerns that have surrounded infant baptism through the centuries, one practical concern immediately presents itself: the individual's lack of choice in the matter. There is no personal conversion experience in infant baptism. Although the hope of subsequent adult ratification normally accompanies the baptism of an infant, the act itself reflects neither a change of heart nor a solemn decision of personal commitment by the child.

Baptism Only Spiritual?

Equally disturbing as any of the above views is the widely-held belief that baptism is not essential at any point in time as part of the Christian experience. Has that been your own understanding? If so, you are not alone. A number of major Christian fellowships neither include baptism as part of their missionary message nor encourage their believers to participate in the act. One's relationship with God is established by the mere acceptance of Jesus Christ as Lord and Savior and the subsequent living of a righteous life pursuant to the teachings of Christ. Baptism is spiritualized as being merely symbolic of one's identity with the death, burial, and resurrection of Jesus.

In taking this view, various fellowships have opted to stress spiritual regeneration and have, in doing so, rejected altogether the importance of water baptism. Perhaps they are reacting to an overemphasis on what historically has been known as "baptismal regeneration"—the idea that, regardless of any other factors, the mere act of baptism results automatically in one's receiving salvation.

The immediate difficulty with dispensing of baptism altogether is the overwhelming scriptural teaching on water baptism and its role in the Christian experience. One can hardly escape the significance of Jesus' own baptism in the Jordan River and His command that baptism be taught and practiced, or the example of the first Christian converts who were baptized in water, or the subsequent apostolic reflections on baptism in their letters to the churches. From Jesus to Peter to Paul, there is a steady stream of biblical emphasis on baptism.

Toward a Better Understanding

In centuries past, baptism has been hotly debated. Conflicting views on baptism have caused major divisions within otherwise cohesive fellowships. The "correct view" of baptism has justified the rightness of one group to the exclusion of all others.

Today, although earlier divisions remain intact, the debates have largely subsided. Each church seems to let others hold their own equally-acceptable views. The only noticeable trend is the emergence of more and more independent churches that call upon their members to consider baptism a significant part of Christian obedience.

What does the future hold for baptism? Will there ever be any substantial agreement about it in the Christian community? Surely this would be the hope of the "one Lord" whose apostles in the "one faith" wrote so confidently of the "one baptism" (Ephesians 4:4-6). And that is the purpose of this book as well.

More importantly, baptism is one of those doctrinal subjects that touches each of us personally. In this life, of course, we may never fully understand the doctrine of the Trinity. We may never get a good handle on such theological terms as *sanctification, justification,* or *atonement.* We can only thank God that, in the world to come, the theology books will be crystal clear to even the most uneducated soul.

By contrast, baptism is an act in which most of us have participated, in one way or another. It is an *experience*—not just an abstract religious idea. Therefore, the question for each of us is: "What is the meaning of baptism in my own life?"

Have you ever stopped to consider why your parents had you baptized? Or why you yourself chose to go through the act? If you have never been baptized, have you ever wondered why so many other people have done it, or why there is so much talk about baptism in the New Testament? Are you interested in knowing what baptism meant for the early Christians and what it means for us now? This book attempts to answer these questions.

Some Housekeeping Before We Begin

Before we launch into a more detailed discussion of the scriptures that relate to baptism, there are some important things to keep in mind along the way.

First, this book primarily addresses *our response* to God's own initiative and offer of salvation. Therefore, the temptation for us might be to humanize an essentially divine process. But any attempt to understand our human response to God's divine grace will be dangerously misguided if we see salvation resulting from *anything* we might do. Salvation is a divine act of mercy, a work of the Spirit. Whatever else it might be, baptism is a *response*. What we know about baptism (something *we* do) must not be divorced from what we know about God (who has already done what we could never do).

Second, the intricate fabric of salvation, which begins and ends with God in Christ, will be the underlying assumption from which the various threads of biblical teaching will be separated out for closer inspection. The danger in viewing each thread of doctrine separately is that salvation may appear to be fragmented and compartmentalized. One may get the idea that we can recognize salvation by a particular process. But in God's sight, our salvation exists when *He* deems it to exist. The most we can do is to attempt a clearer picture of the various ways in which God has called us to respond to His grace.

Third, it is often easy to assume that what God would have us do in response to Him is expressed in general biblical themes, such as faith and love, without carefully searching the Scriptures to see whether that assumption is correct. Therefore, a deliberate attempt has been made to focus on individual verses of Scripture rather than to rely on more broad-sweeping themes. But this approach has its own risk—that we can get so focused on particular passages relating to baptism that we lose sight of that which remains ultimately important—the dynamic process of salvation itself.

Finally, there is no escape from the format of this book, including as it does detailed scriptural analysis and reasoned argument. Nor, typically, is baptism a subject that lends itself to fluffy presentation or popular reading. But it is hoped that the analogy used throughout this book will be a refreshing new way to approach a topic that for too long has been relegated to dry theological tomes.

Reflections

1. If baptism does not keep one from future sin, of what value is it?

2. In what ways is baptism more than simply an act of obedience?

3. What practical implications flow from being baptized either "into the church" or "into Christ"?

4. Can baptism ever be a means whereby we merit salvation?

5. What danger lies in thinking of baptism as part of a "formula" which results in salvation?

6. For what wrong reasons might people choose to be baptized?

7. What statement is being made when one is baptized "after being saved"?

8. What statement is being made when one is baptized "for the forgiveness of sin"?

9. If you have been baptized, what has baptism meant to your life?

10. If you have not been baptized, have you considered why baptism gets so much attention in the New Testament?

CHAPTER 2

The Wedding Ceremony of Baptism

> "Since baptism to Christ is baptism to his death and resurrection, the most critical experiences that human beings can know after birth, namely death and resurrection, have already happened to the baptized!"
>
> G. R. Beasley-Murray

How do we begin to sort out the confusion in the Christian community about the necessity, meaning, form, and timing of Christian baptism? How can you and I get a handle on what the experience of baptism is intended to mean to us?

I would like to suggest a picture that can help us see more clearly the significance and beauty of baptism. The picture is of a wedding ceremony, which formalizes the lifetime commitment of love between a man and a woman. Drawing as it does from traditional weddings in our own twentieth-century Western culture, it is not a picture that comes directly from Scripture. Even so, in several passages, the picture of baptism as a wedding ceremony is vividly suggested.

Naturally, all human attempts to clarify the spiritual dimension suffer from a lack of precision. All human pictures ultimately fail to convey the sublime significance of spiritual concepts. But I think you will be surprised how much of the confusion about baptism can be eliminated by the use of this simple picture. Whether it is a true analogy or is more like an allegory or just a working model for us to use as a jumping-off point in our search for baptism's true meaning, the picture presents compelling new insights. Seeing baptism as a wedding ceremony allows us to reflect perhaps more deeply than ever before on this loving act of covenant with God.

The picture is suggested in a number of biblical contexts. For example, the Lord himself claimed the church as His bride. And here, "the church" is not to be thought of simply in the universal corporate sense. Paul, for instance, told the Christians in Corinth: "I promised you to one husband, to Christ, so that I might present you as a pure virgin to him" (2 Corinthians 11:2). If we are individually and collectively the bride of Christ, it is reasonable to ask: "When did we become the bride, and through what ceremony? In what way have we pledged our love and commitment to Christ, and He to us? By what act of covenant have we joined our lives to His?"

In pursuing this analogy, and even more so the more detailed picture it suggests, we start with the institution of the marriage relationship. In the beginning, when God created man and woman, He joined them together in the union of flesh and spirit that we know as marriage:

> The man said,
> "This is now bone of my bones
>   and flesh of my flesh;
> she shall be called 'woman,'
>   for she was taken out of man."
> For this reason a man will leave his father and mother and be united to his wife, and they will become one flesh (Genesis 2:23, 24).

Underscoring the permanence of the marriage relationship, Jesus added the words that now frequently conclude a wedding ceremony: "So they are no longer two, but one. Therefore what God has joined together, let man not separate" (Matthew 19:6). In marriage, the husband and wife form a perfect complement, two persons united as one—in body, in spirit, and in purpose.

In much the same way, Christ takes the church as His own bride, thereby joining body to body so that, thus united, the church becomes *His* body. The church is not to be thought of as an institution or organization, but as the universal, collective body of individual Christians that has existed throughout the ages. In assuring us of this fact, Paul also gives us our first indication of the role baptism plays in our becoming part of Christ's body:

> The body is a unit, though it is made up of many parts; and though all its parts are many, they form one body. So it is with Christ. *For we were all baptized by one Spirit into one body*—whether Jews or Greeks, slave or free—and we were all given the one Spirit to drink (1 Corinthians 12:12-14).

Paul tells us clearly that our union in one body with Christ takes place *individually,* when we are baptized by the power of the Spirit. Although Paul's reference to our "baptism" by the Spirit may refer primarily to the divine act of regeneration on God's part, we will see how our own baptism in water is associated with God's act of grace.

The beauty of picturing baptism as a wedding ceremony is best seen in Paul's sublime explanation of how Christ loves His church—as His bride. Just when one thinks that the passage is intended as instruction for husbands in their relationship with their wives, Paul turns the message into a mystical, profound reference to Christ and the church. And by quoting the words from Genesis which first instituted marriage, Paul draws ever closer to the Biblical analogy.

> In this same way, husbands ought to love their wives as their own bodies. He who loves his wife loves himself. After all, no one ever hated his own body, but he feeds and cares for it, just as Christ does the church—for we are members of his body. "For this reason a man will leave his father and mother and be united to his wife, and the two will become one flesh." *This is a profound mystery—but I am talking about Christ and the church* (Ephesians 5:28,32).

While Paul unquestionably found a significant tie between marriage and Christ's relationship with Christians, the serendipity is that, in the preceding verses, he also extended the analogy to the wedding itself. By Jewish custom (as seen, for example, in Ezekiel 23:40), the bride would bathe herself in an act of ceremonial cleansing before donning her wedding dress and putting on special ornaments that were worn for the occasion. Similarly, in modern times, the bride traditionally wears a white wedding gown to signify the purity she brings to her bridegroom.

Christ is acutely aware that we are not pure brides. Not one of us is without sin. Therefore, Christ cleanses us and makes us pure as He brings us into a loving relationship with himself. To describe that cleansing, Paul brings us directly to the wedding ceremony of baptism:

> Husbands, love your wives, just as Christ loved the church and gave himself up for her to make her holy, cleansing her by the washing with water through the word, and to present her to himself as a radiant church, without stain or wrinkle or any other blemish, but holy and blameless (Ephesians 5:25-27).

As Christians, we have been washed in the waters of baptism to be a pure bride for Christ.

On one occasion, Paul reminisced about his personal, dramatic conversion experience and the purpose of his own baptism. He said that Ananias had told him: "And now what are you waiting for? Get up, be baptized and *wash your sins away,* calling on his name" (Acts 22:16). It is the same for each of us. With the water of baptism, the bridegroom washes away our sins, bathes us in his own purity, and presents us to himself as a righteous bride.

Could we ever, through our own efforts, be able to present ourselves pure and free from sin? Never! Therefore, when we act on our faith in God's Word and submit to being washed by Christ in the water of baptism, our cleansing is solely a matter of God's grace and mercy. Paul emphasized this point in his letter to Titus when he referred to our rebirth through the washing and renewal of our spirit:

> But when the kindness and love of God our Savior appeared, he saved us, not because of righteous things we had done, *but because of his mercy. He saved us through the washing of rebirth and renewal by the Holy Spirit,* whom he poured out on us generously through Jesus Christ our Savior, so that, having been *justified by his grace,* we might become heirs having the hope of eternal life (Titus 3:4-7).

Neither Water Nor Spirit Alone

Paul's letter to Titus introduced the Holy Spirit as the source of our own spiritual regeneration, which takes place in the act of water baptism. Paul earlier had said we are "baptized by one Spirit into one body" (1 Corinthians 12:13). Here he says we experience "renewal by the Holy Spirit." In his well-known conversation with Nicodemus, Jesus explained how the water and the Spirit combine to bring about one's spiritual rebirth:

> . . . Jesus declared, "I tell you the truth, no one can see the kingdom of God unless he is born again."
>
> "How can a man be born when he is old?" Nicodemus asked. "Surely he cannot enter a second time into his mother's womb to be born!"
>
> Jesus answered, "I tell you the truth, *no one can enter the kingdom of God unless he is born of water*

> *and the Spirit.* Flesh gives birth to flesh, but the Spirit
> gives birth to spirit" (John 3:3-6).

When Jesus said that we must be "born of water and the Spirit," we first might assume that the "water" has some connection with our physical birth into *this* world and that the rebirth of the Spirit refers to the spiritual transformation of life that prepares us for *the world to come.* This antithetical contrast is a particularly tempting perspective since it parallels what Jesus said about flesh giving birth to flesh and Spirit giving birth to spirit. But there appears to be an even greater significance to Jesus' use of the word *water,* which, after all, is not the first word one is likely to think of in reference to the birth process.

Nicodemus realized almost to the point of irritation that Jesus had to be talking about something other than a natural, physical birth "of water" by which each of us has already entered into this world. He knew that repeating our natural birth is impossible. A second look reveals that Jesus is telling us how we enter *the kingdom* when He calls us to be born of water as well as of the Spirit. Both the "water" of baptism and the divine initiative of the "Spirit" are involved in our supernatural, spiritual rebirth.

Jesus was in a unique position to teach us that our spiritual rebirth comes exclusively from the Holy Spirit. After all, His own physical life in this world began when He was miraculously conceived in Mary's womb, also exclusively by the power of the Holy Spirit. When we are born again in Christ, it is the *Holy Spirit* moving in our lives that regenerates us, not merely the external ritual of water baptism. All the ritual in the world could not save us, as those who went to John for baptism quickly learned. John demanded repentance—a new, born-again heart in submission to God—on the part of those being baptized.

In Jesus' discussion about the ritual use of water and how it occasions a person's spiritual cleansing, Jesus may well be alluding to Ezekiel's picture of God's restoring the broken people of Israel after their great spiritual fall:

'I will sprinkle clean water on you, and you will be clean; I will cleanse you from all your impurities and from all your idols. I will give you a new heart and put a new spirit in you; I will remove from you your heart of stone and give you a heart of flesh. And I will put my Spirit in you and move you to follow my decrees and be careful to keep my laws (Ezekiel 36:25-27).

Along with the outer cleansing by ritual water must come an inner cleansing of the heart. Water alone— whether the ablutions of Old Testament ritual or the water of Christian baptism—could never substitute for the inner working of the Spirit. Yet, as if to underscore Jesus' reference to the role of water in our spiritual re-generation, John's Gospel takes the reader immediately to Jesus in the Judean countryside where His disciples were busy baptizing—in water—those who believed in Jesus. If an inner cleansing is the true objective, water is nevertheless important as a ritual mode through which the Holy Spirit has chosen to operate.

Many people take great offense at the suggestion that water has anything to do with salvation. Are we really saved by so elementary an element as water? Of course, nothing in Jesus' conversation with Nicodemus suggests that the *water* of baptism puts one into the kingdom. Rather, what puts one into the kingdom is the transformation of spirit that leads the believer to appreciate the significance of water baptism as a loving and obedient response to the Spirit's gracious initiative.

The key to our response to Christ is the *faith* that would lead us to be baptized. Jesus' words to Nicodemus explaining this truth have become one of the most memorized verses in all the Bible: "For God so loved the world that he gave his one and only Son, that whoever believes in him shall not perish but have eternal life" (John 3:16).

And what of those who do not believe? Jesus says, "Whoever does not believe stands condemned . . ." (John 3:18). If one is unwilling to believe in Jesus, the absence of a faith-responsive baptism doesn't call for further condemnation. Baptism makes sense only in the context of obedient faith. The kind of faith that will motivate a person to respond to the call of baptism is the kind of faith that leads to eternal life.

Christian baptism was not the first faith experience in which there was an effectual interaction of water and the Spirit. While warning the Corinthian Christians not to take their salvation lightly, as did their forefathers in the wilderness, Paul recalls for them how their ancestors had been delivered from bondage and from destruction by the overtaking Egyptian army:

> For I do not want you to be ignorant of the fact, brothers, that our forefathers were all under the cloud and that they all passed through the sea. *They were all baptized into Moses in the cloud and in the sea* (1 Corinthians 10:1, 2).

It takes little symbolic insight to see in "the cloud" the working of the Holy Spirit guiding the Israelites in their transition from bondage to freedom. As a nation, they were identified with Moses and regenerated with every courageous step they took while surrounded by the water of the Red Sea, which itself had been parted by God's saving grace.

Acknowledging His Headship

The Israelites' baptism had symbolically put them "into Moses"—that is, under his spiritual leadership. Our baptism puts us into Christ. "You are all sons of God through faith in Christ Jesus," Paul wrote, *"for all of you who were baptized into Christ have clothed yourselves with Christ"* (Galatians 3:26, 27).

Having been baptized into the body of Christ, we also accept His headship, or spiritual leadership, in our lives.

"And God placed all things under his feet and *appointed him to be head over everything for the church, which is his body,* the fullness of him who fills everything in every way" (Ephesians 1:22, 23).

This brings us back to the wedding analogy. In his admonition to wives to submit to the spiritual leadership of their husbands, Paul once again pictured the marriage of Christ and His bride, the church. "Wives, submit to your husbands as to the Lord. For the husband is the head of the wife *as Christ is the head of the church, his body, of which he is the Savior*" (Ephesians 5:22, 23).

In the wedding ceremony of baptism, we not only become united with Christ in His body, but we submit to His spiritual leadership. As the bride of Christ, we covenant to love, honor, *and* submit.

Former Covenants and Symbolic Baptisms

It may seem that we are about to take an unnecessary detour. But, because a wedding ceremony is the initiation of a covenant of love and commitment between the bride and the groom, we need to explore the concept of covenant as revealed in the Bible.

In the most dramatic baptism the world has ever known, God first covenanted with man through the experience of Noah and the flood. God's next covenant came through the promise to Abraham that, through his offspring, all the nations of the earth would be blessed—a covenant to which Abraham responded with the sacrifice of various animals as God commanded.

The promise of a great nation's coming through Abraham's descendants was fulfilled by the birth of the nation of Israel. But the promise of God's blessing to all nations would only be fulfilled centuries later in the coming of the promised Messiah, Jesus.

To say that God "covenanted" with Abraham is somewhat misleading, since a covenant normally requires two parties who are equally capable of making a mutual agreement. Neither Abraham nor any other person could

29

claim equality with God or assume that he or she had anything of value to offer as consideration for the privilege of covenanting with God.

Therefore, the covenant with Abraham was a matter of grace—a unilateral act on the part of God, if you will. In return for His promise, however, God did expect His spiritual children to live righteous lives worthy of the promise.

As a sign of the covenant God made with Abraham, God commanded that newborn male children be circumcised. This unusual rite, administered by the parent on behalf of the child, was ordained as an act of obedience and as a statement of faith in the one God. Circumcision was both a *symbol* of faith and an essential *requirement* of the covenant.

Between the time of the covenant with Abraham and the coming of the promised Messiah, the laws of Moses became the basis for an intermediate covenant. This covenant more closely resembled a covenant of mutuality. The law set forth the ground rules for conduct befitting the people of God. The Israelites' obedience to the law reflected their commitment to the covenant.

God promised that, if the Israelites obeyed the law, He would be their God and they would be His people: *"Now if you obey me fully and keep my covenant, then out of all nations you will be my treasured possession"* (Exodus 19:5, 6). Under the covenant, obedience brought blessings, but disobedience—that is, breaches of the covenant—brought curses.

Premier among all of the laws was the command: "You shall have no other gods before me" (Exodus 20:3). When the law was first given, and on a number of later occasions, the people responded to that command and exchanged their vows, as it were, promising to be faithful to the one God.

Just as in a wedding ceremony, when the bride and groom promise to keep themselves only to each other and to remain faithful, the Israelites exchanged their vows of faithfulness to God: "When Moses went and told the people all the Lord's words and laws, they responded with one voice, *'Everything the Lord has said we will do'"* (Exodus 24:3).

Throughout His covenant relationship with Israel, God continually referred to Israel as His bride whom He had lovingly chosen from among all other people. That this God, as a loving bridegroom, had set His affection on the Israelites and promised to be faithful to them was the subject of this poignant reminder by Moses (Deuteronomy 7:6, 9):

> For you are a people holy to the Lord your God. The Lord your God has chosen you out of all the peoples on the face of the earth to be his people, his treasured possession. . .
> Know therefore that the Lord your God is God; he is the faithful God, keeping his covenant of love to a thousand generations of those who love him and keep his commands.

What bride could wish for a more committed promise from the one she loves? And as a demonstration of covenant love, what could be more important than the knowledge that, through the coming of Jesus, God did indeed fulfill His promise to Abraham and, through him, to the whole world?

The Bride's Covenant With Christ

With the coming of the Messiah, Jesus, there came an altogether new covenant, superior in every way to the covenant of the Jews under the law of Moses. The new covenant did not require the sacrifices that accompanied both the covenant with Abraham and the covenant with the Israelites. It was accomplished once and for all time by the blood of Christ shed in His death on the cross:

> The blood of goats and bulls and the ashes of a heifer sprinkled on those who are ceremonially unclean sanctify them so that they are outwardly clean.

> *How much more, then, will the blood of Christ, who through the eternal Spirit offered himself unblemished to God, cleanse our consciences from acts that lead to death,* so that we may serve the living God! (Hebrews 9:13, 14).

Our own covenant relationship with Christ finds its way back to the wedding ceremony of baptism. For it is in our baptism, says Paul, that we join in Jesus' death:

> *Or don't you know that all of us who were baptized into Christ Jesus were baptized into his death?* We were therefore buried with him through baptism into death in order that, just as Christ was raised from the dead through the glory of the Father, we too may live a new life (Romans 6:3, 4).

Because the new covenant was bought and paid for by the blood of Jesus Christ, we have this in common with those who were earlier in covenant relationship with God: the wedding of Christ and the church is a joining of unequals.

Baptism Is the New Sign of Covenant

It's exciting to know that through Christ we have a transcendent and superior covenant! But because we are searching out the significance of the act of baptism, there is even more good news. Our new covenant relationship is initiated by a new sign, a new rite of purification. And it is baptism! With what must have been a sense of relief, Paul tells us that our baptism into Christ is now the physical mark of our new circumcision—the perfect picture of putting off a sinful nature through a washing done by Christ's own hand:

> In him you were also circumcised, in the putting off of the sinful nature, not with a circumcision done by the hands of men but with the circumcision done by Christ, having been buried with him in baptism and raised with him through your faith in the power of God, who raised him from the dead (Colossians 2:11, 12)

Circumcision was a symbol involving physical pain that initiated one to the bondage of law, while baptism is a symbol of joyful entrance into the welcome yoke of marriage with Christ. Circumcision was a symbol of exclusivity, covenanting God's special love with one nation of people, while baptism is the symbol of God's universal love extended to every individual in every nation, race, and culture throughout all time.

But there is this warning. If anyone believes that, by simply going through the external motions of baptism, he has entered into covenant relationship with Christ, he is fooling himself. As Peter said, baptism is "not the removal of dirt from the body but the pledge of a good conscience toward God" (1 Peter 3:21). The true significance of baptism is not what happens on the outside of the package. It's what happens on the inside that makes the outer act important.

What purpose would be served by a wedding if there were no loving relationship between the bride and the groom? Or if there were no real commitment? It would be a sham wedding. When an annulment is granted on this basis, it recognizes that the *ritual* did not result in a valid marriage. So it is with baptism if the ritual is not motivated by sincere intention and commitment.

If there is no creation of a new spirit, baptism is an empty gesture and an affront to Christ. But when the wedding ceremony of baptism is entered into lovingly, with faith and commitment, it becomes—by God's grace—the entrance into a new covenant relationship with Christ.

Importance of Baptism

Through the words of Scripture, we have viewed the Christian's relationship to Christ as a marriage in which faith-responsive baptism is the wedding ceremony. The very heart of the gospel message is that the blessings which attach to the act of baptism are made possible only through a new and superior covenant of grace sealed by the blood of Christ. What we have seen, clearly and simply, is that God has joined together the gospel and baptism. "Therefore what God has joined together, let man not separate."

Reflections

1. If the church collectively is the bride of Christ, how are we *individually* the bride?

2. How does the love relationship between a man and a woman relate to their wedding ceremony?

3. In what ways is the covenant relationship in marriage like our covenant relationship with God?

4. What significance attached to the rituals surrounding the covenants with Abraham and the nation of Israel?

5. How does the ritual of baptism symbolize the covenant between God and the believer today?

6. What pledge is being made through the act of baptism?

7. What role does water play in the believer's covenant with God?

8. What is the true source of our cleansing?

9. If it is what's on the inside that counts most, can the outer ritual be dispensed with without spiritual consequences?

10. What covenant have *you* made with God?

CHAPTER 3

A RESPLENDENT WEDDING

"Through the visible as a school we rise up to the appreciation of the invisible."

F. W. Robertson

A Divine Proposal

In what other religion has God descended from His throne in heaven and asked us to be united with Him in His glory? In other religions, man tries to reach God through his own efforts—reaching up, reaching out, reaching within, reaching in vain for what he could never hope to attain. In Christianity, God himself breaks through into our own lives. It is God who reaches down for us. No, it's even better than that. He comes to us in our own world. In the person of Jesus, He became like us so that we could become like Him.

As we read the Scriptures and see the truth of the gospel working in our lives, we are drawn inexorably into a relationship with Christ. The "dating" stage leads comfortably and easily into a mental commitment—an "engagement"—to become one with Christ. When we fall in love with Christ's character and goodness, we naturally want to respond to Jesus' invitation. Coming as it does from Christ himself, it is a proposal of unparalleled majesty.

The "Best Man" of Repentance

The scripturally-suggested picture of baptism as a wedding ceremony, in which Christ takes us to be His holy bride, exists in many surprising details. One detail is presented to us by John the Baptist, whose own ministry was so closely tied to the act of baptism that we remember him as "the baptizer." John referred to himself as the friend of the bridegroom. As we might put it today, John was Jesus' "best man" for the wedding.

John's role as "best man" is seen in the very message he preached. That message was a call for repentance. And ironically, the message of repentance—like John the Baptist himself—is a forerunner leading to Christ.

In the time of Christ, the "friend of the bridegroom" made all the necessary arrangements for the wedding on behalf of the bridegroom. He was to make certain that everything was ready for the ceremony. If there were any problems, he was to resolve them. In much the same way, repentance identifies problems that stand in the way of one's relationship with Christ and prompts any needed personal changes.

Repentance is a changed-life response growing out of the regret we feel for the life we have lived without submitting to Christ's lordship. For some, repentance may require a 180-degree turn in daily actions, prompted by remorse for sin. This penitent attitude and willingness to be transformed is at the core of our baptism. It prepares the way for the salvation to come. Isaiah prophesied about John the Baptist and repentance:

> "A voice of one calling in the desert,
> 'Prepare the way for the Lord,
>   make straight paths for him.
> Every valley shall be filled in,

> every mountain and hill made low.
> The crooked roads shall become straight,
>   the rough ways smooth.
> And all mankind will see God's salvation'"
>   (Luke 3:4-6; cf. Isaiah 40:3-5).

In the process of repenting, we take measure of our lives and admit that we are lacking. Repentance is a time of spiritual reflection that calls us to be painfully honest and to see the need to straighten out our lives— the need to make the rough ways smooth. Repentance is the willingness to let Christ fill our emptiness and lead us in new directions. Without this compliant attitude, we will never enjoy God's salvation.

Recall for a moment the traditional words of the minister at the beginning of a wedding ceremony: "If you or anyone in this assembly knows any just cause why this marriage should not be performed, let him speak now or forever hold his peace." If one is not *qualified,* he is not ready to be *solemnized* in a ceremony that memorializes such a commitment. The heart must be prepared for its salvation.

Songs for the Celebration

What would a wedding be without music? In writing his letter of encouragement to the young evangelist Timothy, Paul refers to a song that many scholars believe was sung on the occasion of a baptism. It refers both to our symbolic association with Christ's death and to the covenant relationship that is confirmed in that watery grave. And it concludes with a beautiful reminder that, even when we are unfaithful, Christ nevertheless will remain faithful to us:

> If we died with him,
>   we will also live with him;
> if we endure,
>   we will also reign with him.

37

> If we disown him,
>   he will also disown us;
> if we are faithless,
>   he will remain faithful,
>   for he cannot disown himself
>   (2 Timothy 2:11-13).

The wedding songs that celebrate our new relationship with Christ will become a permanent part of the life we have in Him. We can, and should, be constantly filled with joyous singing in our hearts. For us, the celebration never ends. Every day is our honeymoon.

The Resplendent Wedding Gown

With the appearance of the bride, the guests excitedly turn to look at her in all her beauty, and at the gown she is wearing for her special moment. As the bride of Christ, we are beautifully clothed in the wedding ceremony of faith-responsive baptism. Paul put it this way: "You are all sons of God *through faith* in Christ Jesus, *for all of you who were baptized into Christ have clothed yourselves with Christ*" (Galatians 3:26, 27).

Even before the coming of Christ and our being clothed with Him in faith and baptism, the prophet Isaiah associated the bride's wedding gown with salvation:

> I delight greatly in the Lord;
>   my soul rejoices in my God.
> *For he has clothed me with garments of salvation*
>   *and arrayed me in a robe of righteousness,*
> as a bridegroom adorns his head like a priest,
>   and as a bride adorns herself with her jewels
>   (Isaiah 61:10).

The righteousness with which we are clothed as we approach Christ is a gift for us to wear. If we were left to our own spiritual wardrobes, of course, we would be clothed in only soiled and wrinkled wedding garments. But the groom knows our spiritual shortcomings and wants us to be radiant in righteousness. So as we walk down the aisle of faith, He surrounds us in the beauty of His own righteousness. Though our lives are tattered and torn, He makes us elegant!

The Great Cloud of Witnesses

The minister traditionally begins the wedding ceremony with the familiar words: "We are gathered together in the presence of God and these witnesses to join this man and this woman in holy matrimony." Sometimes the assembled "crowd" is limited to the one or two witnesses required by law. Perhaps just a friend of the bride and a friend of the groom or the sweet old couple who accommodate impulse marriages in an all-night wedding chapel in Las Vegas. More often the crowd is composed of the many friends and relatives who have come to share in this moment of joyous celebration.

Witnessing a wedding ceremony is not only a joyful experience, but it is also a factor contributing to the solemnity of the occasion. The public sharing of the couple's commitment lends credibility to the marriage vows. The presence of witnesses eliminates any question about the legitimacy of the relationship.

The wedding ceremony of baptism is not a private affair to be done in a corner. It is a public declaration of our commitment to God. Dietrich Bonhoeffer said it well:

> When he called men to follow him, Jesus was summoning them to a *visible act of obedience.* To follow Jesus was a public act. Baptism is similarly a public event, for it is the means whereby a member is grafted on to the visible body of Christ *(Cost of Discipleship, p. 259).*

While the Communion is a visible, public reminder of Christ's sacrificial death, baptism is a visible, public reminder that the believer himself is putting to death his old nature. We must not forget that, while baptism expresses our own commitment to Christ, our actual union with Christ and our grafting into the invisible body of Christ is accomplished by the Holy Spirit. We must never confuse ceremony with substance, human response with divine initiative.

There is another kind of witnessing taking place as well. In the formality of a wedding—no matter how simple—a timeless, universal message is being proclaimed. The couple proclaims to the whole world that there is something important about two people's committing their lives to each other in love.

In baptism, several statements are also being made. One message is that there is something important about being united together with Jesus Christ. Another message—seen in baptism's visual imagery—is that Christ's death, burial, and resurrection transforms our lives while on this earth. Only through Christ's sacrificial death upon the cross are our sins forgiven. And through the power of Jesus' resurrection, we learn of the power He brings to our otherwise hopeless situation.

Still another message proclaimed through the act of baptism is suggested in a difficult passage that speaks of how baptism is a testimony to the world about our confident assurance of life after death. Paul wrote, *"Now if there is no resurrection, what will those do who are baptized for the dead? If the dead are not raised at all, why are people baptized for them?"* (1 Corinthians 15:29).

It appears that Paul used a known practice of his day for the sake of argument, without actually approving of the concept of vicarious salvation that the practice would imply. He makes the important point that baptism symbolizes not only Jesus' resurrection, but also the great resurrection in which we will all be participants. Baptism proclaims our own resurrection!

The Sacred Vows

Perhaps the most important part of any wedding ceremony is the exchange of vows between the bride and the groom. Certainly the commitment to marriage will have preceded the ceremony itself, with the spoken intentions of (typically) the man who has proposed and the woman who has accepted the proposal. There is an implicit agreement in the couple's engagement regarding the ultimate direction in which their relationship is headed. But until the vows are exchanged, either party is free to change his or her mind and not commit further to a lifetime together.

In the wedding ceremony, the groom typically promises to love, honor, and protect the bride. The bride traditionally promises to love, honor, and cherish the man she is taking in marriage. Both promise to remain faithful to each other until death do them part, which are terribly serious words in a throwaway world. For Christians, the marriage covenant should be the second most important commitment they will ever make.

The most important commitment anyone will make is the commitment of one's life to Christ. And that total submission is expressed as a pledge in the wedding ceremony of baptism. Peter talks about that pledge in comparing the floodwaters that saved Noah through the faith -act of baptism:

> . . . God waited patiently in the days of Noah while the ark was being built. In it only a few people, eight in all, were saved through water, and this water symbolizes baptism that now saves you also—not the removal of dirt from the body but *the pledge of a good conscience toward God* (1 Peter 3:20, 21).

The flood, in which the lives of only eight people were saved, was symbolic of a much greater salvation—a spiritual cleansing available to all mankind. Baptism, as a wedding pledge, is the outward, open, tangible, and public expression of one's acceptance of Christ's offer of love and spiritual union. Through the act of baptism, we come before "a great cloud of witnesses" and pledge to Christ our love and commitment.

Baptism, as a public act of obedience and commitment, is itself a confession of one's faith in Christ. Beyond that, the first Christians accompanied the act of baptism with actual spoken confessions of their faith in Christ. Apparently, it was done in very much the same fashion as the vows made by a wedding couple. Paul seems to refer to these public confessions when he reminded his protege Timothy of his pledge of commitment to Christ: "Take hold of the eternal life to which you were called when you made your good confession in the presence of many witnesses" (1 Timothy 6:12).

Paul's advice to Timothy expresses the value of making a public, oral confession of faith and engaging in the visible pledge that baptism represents. Public acts of commitment bolster one's inner resolve and, in times of weakness, provide a tangible point of reference from which to draw strength.

This commitment must not be entered into lightly. No vow—especially one of commitment to Christ—should be made without prayerful consideration of the potential implications. In marriage, for example, there will be not only good times to share, but also bad times to endure together.

One of the symbolic statements made by baptism is that we are joining Christ in His suffering. Jesus fully disclosed this ever-present reality when He rebuked His disciples for wanting the benefits of discipleship without the burdens:

> Then James and John, the sons of Zebedee, came to him. "Teacher," they said, "we want you to do for us whatever we ask."
>
> "What do you want me to do for you?" he asked.
>
> They replied, "Let one of us sit at your right and the other at your left in your glory."
>
> "You don't know what you are asking," Jesus said. "Can you drink the cup I drink *or be baptized with the baptism I am baptized with?*"
>
> "We can," they answered [quite unaware of how they would indeed suffer as Christians!] (Mark 10:35-39).

No bride or groom wants to anticipate problems that will threaten physical or emotional well-being. So it is unlikely, during the wedding ceremony, that much serious reflection accompanies the call for commitment "in sickness and in health."

Likewise, none of us wants to anticipate suffering for being a Christian. But suffer we will, and suffer we do. In the wedding ceremony of baptism, we tie our destiny to Christ—whether that leads us to joy and peace or to persecution and suffering.

Sealed by the Ring of the Spirit

Analogies tempt us to reach beyond reasonable comparisons and here we may risk that danger. But a passage in Paul's second letter to the Corinthians suggests that yet another detail of the wedding ceremony is involved in the act of baptism. One of the central features of a wedding is the exchange of rings. The rings are symbols of the purity, preciousness, and durability of the relationship. They also are tokens of the vows that are made.

In earlier times, when the bride was considered as much a property interest as a love partner, the ring given by the husband was a token of his loving "possession" of the bride. Perhaps it may be said that the "seal of possession" corresponds to the role of the wedding ring. This analogy comes even closer in light of the fact that ancient seals often were attached to rings:

> Now it is God who makes both us and you stand firm in Christ. He anointed us, *set his seal of ownership on us,* and put his Spirit in our hearts as a deposit, guaranteeing what is to come (2 Corinthians 1:21, 22).

Just as wedding rings represent durability, Paul says we have been sealed with the Holy Spirit as against all future contingencies. Our spiritual wedding ring tells the world that we have received unbreakable promises through the Holy Spirit. Paul reiterated this idea in his letter to the Ephesians:

> Having believed, you were marked in him with a seal, the promised Holy Spirit, who is a deposit guaranteeing our inheritance until the redemption of those who are God's possession—to the praise of his glory (Ephesians 1:13, 14).

When the husband in a temporal wedding places his ring on the bride's finger as a seal of his promises to her, he cannot guarantee her a marriage free of disappointment. But through our obedient faith, accepting the working of the Holy Spirit, we can be assured that in the day of redemption Christ will acknowledge us as His bride and proudly carry us across the threshold of heaven.

Thinking of the Spirit as only the "ring" sealing our relationship to Christ would separate the many interwoven threads of salvation. God's Holy Spirit both initiates our new relationship and seals its success. That which comes last is that which has already come first. It is the Spirit who causes us to be aware of our sin and our need of forgiveness. It is the Spirit who points us to Jesus Christ as the way. And it is the Spirit who gives us the assurance that we are accepted.

From beginning to end, our salvation is the work of the Spirit reconciling us to God. Faith and baptism are our loving response to what the Spirit has already done for us.

God Is the Minister

When the songs have been sung, the vows repeated, and the rings exchanged, there comes the magical moment that brings the ceremony to its happy conclusion. Only one who has performed a wedding ceremony can know the joy that comes when proudly pronouncing the happy couple to be husband and wife. That pronouncement is prefaced with words to this effect: "By the authority vested in me by the state, and as a minister of the gospel, I now pronounce you husband and wife."

In the wedding ceremony of baptism, the person performing the rite is also careful to preface the act with an appeal to the proper authority, as set forth in Jesus' commission to His apostles:

> Then Jesus came to them and said, "All authority in heaven and on earth has been given to me. Therefore go and make disciples of all nations, baptizing them in the name of the Father and of the Son and of the Holy Spirit, and teaching them to obey everything I have commanded you" (Matthew 28:18-20).

Whether it be a wedding or a baptism, it is not simply a matter of uttering words of ritual tradition. In order to be officially recognized by the state, the married couple must comply with the requirements concerning a license, witnesses, perhaps blood tests, and ministerial capacity. Likewise, it is only by the authority of the one triune God that our relationship with Christ is given official recognition. His divine authority is being recognized when one is baptized in the name of the Father, the Son, and the Holy Spirit.

We must be careful, of course, to distinguish between divine authority and ritual formality. At least two major fellowships literally baptize the believer three times—once in the name of the Father, again in the name of the Son, and a third time in the name of the Holy Spirit! In other fellowships, some question the validity of a single baptism if the exact incantation isn't uttered: "I baptize you in the name of the Father, the Son, and the Holy Spirit."

Surprisingly, those who were baptized on Pentecost were told to be baptized "in the name of Jesus Christ" (Acts 2:38). And Peter also ordered that Cornelius be baptized "in the name of Jesus Christ" (Acts 10:48). The Samaritans, too, were baptized "into the name of the Lord Jesus" (Acts 8:16). Thus, there is little biblical concern for a particular formula in the wording, but there is much concern with the authority from which it proceeds.

David Lloyd-George said, "The church I belong to is torn in a fierce dispute. One section says that baptism is *in* the name of the Father, and the other that it is *into* the name of the Father. I belong to one of these parties. I feel most strongly about it. I would die for it in fact—but I forget which it is!" Words may either contribute to our understanding or obscure the obvious.

Naturally, the person administering baptism proceeds under God's authority. He is acting solely as God's agent in facilitating the ceremony. A clearer understanding of this principle might have prevented a problem that arose in the Corinthian church and stubbornly persists in the Christian community even today. In his first letter to the Corinthians, the apostle Paul rebuked them for a sectarian spirit that had divided them. Oddly, it stemmed from their allegiance to those who were instrumental in their conversion. They were confusing the groom, to whom they had been united in the wedding ceremony of baptism, with the minister, who had performed the ceremony!

One claimed to follow Apollos, perhaps because Apollos had brought him to know the gospel (and may even have baptized him). Another claimed to follow Cephas, perhaps because Cephas had brought him to know the gospel. (There is no evidence that Cephas—Peter—was ever in Corinth to convert any of the Corinthians, but he may have brought some of them to Christ in some other place. Then, too, his being one of the original apostles may have been seen by some as a reason to give him more authority or honor.)

You can almost see Paul, red-faced with anger, as he writes to point out the obvious misconception:

> One of you says, "I follow Paul"; another, "I follow Apollos"; another, "I follow Cephas"; still another, "I follow Christ."
> *Is Christ divided? Was Paul crucified for you? Were you baptized into the name of Paul?* I am thankful that

> I did not baptize any of you except Crispus and Gaius, so no one can say that you were baptized into my name. (Yes, I also baptized the household of Stephanas; beyond that, I don't remember if I baptized anyone else.) *For Christ did not send me to baptize, but to preach the gospel* —not with words of human wisdom, lest the cross of Christ be emptied of its power (1 Corinthians 1:12-17).

When Paul says he was not sent to baptize, he is not telling us he doesn't believe baptism is important. He personally baptized at least a few of the Corinthian Christians. And he is indicating that the other Christians in Corinth had been taught and baptized by someone. What Paul is stating in no uncertain terms is that the person actually doing the converting or the baptizing is not important.

The believer's baptism is solely by the authority of the triune God of Heaven—not by any human authority. Christ alone died for our sins. And it is into His name alone that we are baptized.

Luke removes any doubt that there is but "one baptism," and that it must be in the name and by the authority of Christ:

> While Apollos was at Corinth, Paul took the road through the interior and arrived at Ephesus. There he found some disciples and asked them, "Did you receive the Holy Spirit when you believed?"
>
> They answered, "No, we have not even heard that there is a Holy Spirit."
>
> So Paul asked, "Then what baptism did you receive?" "John's baptism," they replied.
>
> Paul said, "John's baptism was a baptism of repentance. He told the people to believe in the one coming after him, that is, in Jesus." *On hearing this, they were baptized into the name of the Lord Jesus* (Acts 19:1-5).

Baptism unassociated with Christ and His unique lordship is of no value. Not just any baptism will do. The fact that baptism is to be done only pursuant to Christ's authority ought to compel us to tread very carefully when observing its requirements.

Name Above All Names

Another exciting point in the traditional wedding ceremony occurs when the bride and groom are presented for the first time as a couple sharing the same name. The minister might say, for example, "It is my pleasure to introduce to you, for the first time, Mr. and Mrs. Peter Jones." And with that happy introduction, the bride will have taken the name of her husband, recognizing thereby his spiritual leadership in their newly-formed relationship.

Similarly, in the wedding ceremony of baptism, we also take the groom's name—the name of Christ—and recognize His spiritual lordship over our lives. Isaiah prophesied beautifully concerning this new name:

> The nations will see your righteousness,
>   and all kings your glory;
> *you will be called by a new name that the*
>   *mouth of the Lord will bestow....*
> For the Lord will take delight in you,
>   and your land will be married.
> As a young man marries a maiden,
>   so will your sons marry you;
> as a bridegroom rejoices over his bride
>   so will your God rejoice over you (Isaiah 62:2-5).

Although the name "Christian" is referred to only three times in Scripture, there is no mystery as to why it is the name we wear. By wearing Christ's name, we proudly announce to the world that we belong to Him and that we share an intimate relationship with Him.

The mystery is why we insist on wearing other names as well! We dishonor the one to whom we have submitted our lives if we insist on labeling ourselves by sectarian names. Like the Corinthians, we have called ourselves, in effect, Apollosites, Cephasites, and Paulites, rather than simply Christians. When someone asks what we are religiously, we too often respond with a denominational name. It's not that we have renounced the name "Christian." We've simply compromised it with the use of a hyphen. Because Christians are baptized into Christ's name alone, Christians alone is what we ought to be.

What's in a name? Heritage, identity, pride, association, reputation, authority, and power. As the bride of Christ, we are entitled to appropriate to ourselves each of these attributes of a name as they find their ultimate meaning in Him. It's what Ananias told Paul he could do as a new creature in Christ: "Get up, be baptized and wash your sins away, *calling on his name*" (Acts 22:16).

As Christians we are honored to wear the most important name the world will ever know—the name of the one who brought the universe into existence, who even now loves and sustains us, and by whom the world one day will be judged.

The Wedding Celebration

We've already seen how the Ethiopian eunuch was baptized and then "went on his way rejoicing." When another convert, the Philippian jailer, was baptized by Paul and Silas, Luke tells us: "The jailer brought them into his house and set a meal before them; he was filled with joy because he had come to believe in God—he and his whole family" (Acts 16:34).

With the wedding ceremony of baptism comes indescribable joy and celebration, not unlike the wedding reception that traditionally follows the marriage ceremony.

There is no happier picture of celebration than in the return of the lost son. The banquet given in his honor is a wonderful reminder of the joy that accompanies the repentance and confession leading one to salvation:

49

> The son said to him, "Father, I have sinned against heaven and against you. I am no longer worthy to be called your son."
>
> But the father said to his servants, "Quick! Bring the best robe and put it on him. Put a ring on his finger and sandals on his feet. Bring the fattened calf and kill it. Let's have a feast and celebrate. For this son of mine was dead and is alive again; he was lost and is found." So they began to celebrate (Luke 15:21-24).

The occasion of a baptism has always been a time of joyous celebration for family and friends in Christ. We should be even more excited knowing that, in our celebration, we are joined by Christ himself and all the heavenly hosts!

Showers of Spiritual Gifts

No wedding is complete without beautifully-wrapped gifts for the bride and groom. With the wedding ceremony of baptism also come many spiritual gifts. The most treasured gifts that could possibly be given are promised at the conclusion of Peter's sermon on Pentecost: "Repent and be baptized, every one of you, in the name of Jesus Christ *for the forgiveness of your sins. And you will receive the gift of the Holy Spirit*" (Acts 2:38, 39).

The first of God's two very special gifts is forgiveness. When we bring the grief of guilt to our baptism, God takes away that grief and replaces it with the joy of forgiveness. What a burden He has taken from our shoulders!

The second of God's very special gifts is the presence of the Holy Spirit in our lives. Forgiven of the sins that separated us from God, we have the continuous power of the Holy Spirit in our lives to bridge the gap between man and God.

We find these two gifts mentioned, almost as if in the same breath, not only in Peter's sermon on Pentecost but also in Paul's letter to the Galatians. *"He redeemed us* in order that the blessing given to Abraham might come to the Gentiles through Christ Jesus, so that by faith we might receive *the promise of the Spirit*" (Galatians 3:14).

John the Baptist also linked these two wonderful gifts when he pointed to Jesus and said, "Look, the Lamb of God, who takes away the sin of the world!" and then testified that it was Jesus Christ who would "baptize with the Holy Spirit" (John 1:29, 33). Forgiveness and the presence of the Holy Spirit—what precious gifts become our spiritual dowry through Christ!

Does that mean that we receive the Holy Spirit apart from the written Word, which was revealed by the Spirit? Absolutely! Certainly our having the gift of the Holy Spirit includes our having the Spirit of Christ within us as an attitude of mind and as a noble spiritual ideal (Romans 8:9-11). But it is more than just that. Paul suggested as much when he asked the Galatian Christians: "Did you receive the Spirit by observing the law, or by believing what you heard?" (Galatians 3:2). Through their faith, the Galatians had *received* something!

The Holy Spirit is not confined to the pages of a book. The Holy Spirit comes into our lives. The Holy Spirit is dynamic and active, powerful and alive. Paul told the Ephesian Christians: "I pray that out of his glorious riches he may strengthen you with power *through his Spirit in your inner being* " (Ephesians 3:16). "Now to him who is able to do immeasurably more than all we ask or imagine, *according to his power that is at work within us,* to him be glory" (Ephesians 3:20).

Almost as if to anticipate our analogy of the wedding ceremony and the gifts that accompany it, Paul links this indwelling of the Spirit to our sonship through faith and baptism: "You are all sons of God through faith in Christ Jesus, for all of you who were baptized into Christ have clothed yourselves with Christ" (Galatians 3:26, 27). "Because you are sons, God sent the Spirit of his Son into our hearts, the Spirit who calls *out, 'Abba,* Father'" (Galatians 4:6).

51

The very idea of God's working within us stretches our understanding to its limits. How we could be given a special relationship with the Creator of the universe, and how His Spirit could interact with ours to bring us all spiritual blessings is indeed a godly mystery. But the promise is clear and unmistakable. And it is altogether wonderful!

Married to Christ!

In the wedding ceremony of baptism, we are brought to Christ by the "best man" of repentance, which turns our lives around and prepares us for the new directions in which Christ will lead us. As joyous wedding songs fill the air, we humbly approach Christ, clothed in the wedding garment of Christ's own righteousness, which He has given us to wear.

In making our public confession of faith, we vow our submission and fidelity to Christ. Even as we say the words, we are aware that it is only through the merciful grace of God that we will be able to honor such vows. Painfully aware of our sinfulness, yet confident of His promise of newness, we pledge our commitment to Christ in this loving act of obedience. As a token of His own love, Christ seals us with the "ring" of the Holy Spirit

Having been united with Christ in baptism by the power and authority of the Father, the Son, and the Holy Spirit, we are greatly honored to be given Christ's own name to wear. In wearing the name "Christian," we proclaim to the whole world our devotion to the one whom we love above all others, and to the one who will continue to love us even when our love wavers.

On this the most important occasion of our lives, the celebration begins on earth, with the family of God into which we are born, and is joined by the angels in heaven, who rejoice at the wonderful news of our salvation. To this banquet of celebration God brings His many spiritual gifts, including the wonderful gift of forgiveness.

And just when we think we have been showered with more blessings than any earthly being deserves, God stops the music, turns up the lights, and announces the greatest gift of all—the gift of His own Holy Spirit within us. A divine presence in our lives. A companion in sickness and in health, in good times and in bad, always for better and never for worse, until death do us bind together for all eternity!

Reflections

1. When did you first feel God wooing you with his love?

2. What has been your experience with repentance, both past and present? Did it require a radical change in lifestyle?

3. What does it mean to be clothed in Christ's righteousness?

4. In what ways do we proclaim a "Christian witness," both in baptism and otherwise?

5. What is the purpose of vows if we are not always true to them, either in spirit or actions?

6. Does baptism lose its symbolic identity with Christ's suffering in a culture where Christians are not faced with persecution?

7. Would Christians perhaps encounter greater persecution if they took the commitment of baptism more seriously?

8. Do you have an ongoing sense that your sins really have been forgiven?

9. Can you identity specific ways in which the Holy Spirit works in your life?

10. What does it mean for you to wear Christ's name?

CHAPTER 4

WHAT'S IN A MARRIAGE?

"The strength of baptism, that's within; It saves the soul from drowning sin."

Robert Herrick

What does it take to make a marriage? When, and under what conditions, are the bride and groom actually joined together in the bond of marriage? Aside from the ceremony, what is the heart, soul, and essence of the marriage relationship?

The same questions may be asked about baptism. What role does baptism play in the conversion process? When do we actually become Christians? Does it happen before we are baptized at the moment of faith, or perhaps when faith is combined with repentance? Is it when we make a personal commitment to accept Jesus Christ as our Lord and Savior? Or do we become Christians only in the process of being baptized, or perhaps even at some later time?

These questions are important because they relate to the purpose, significance, and timing of baptism. For example, if one becomes a Christian at some point prior to baptism, then baptism is more symbol than substance.

To that extent, it becomes less essential, less critical. We have already seen that significant consequences attach to the act of baptism itself, wholly apart from the other elements of conversion.

In the act of baptism we are "buried" with Christ, and we are "baptized into his death" (Romans 6:3, 4). This result is made possible, of course, by the behind-the-scenes work of the Holy Spirit, who, in reality, is doing the baptizing. Paul tied together what the *Holy Spirit* is doing with what *we* are doing when he stated that we are buried with Christ *"through* baptism" (Romans 6:4).

When we are baptized into Christ, we also clothe ourselves with Christ. Simply, but significantly, Paul tells us we are "baptized into Christ Jesus" (Romans 6:3). And, just as in Paul's baptism, it is through baptism that our own sins are washed away. If Paul is right about baptism, it is crucial. But crucial to what? Obedience? Faithfulness? Possibly even to salvation? Albert Schweitzer explained it this way:

> It is with baptism that the being-in-Christ and the dying and rising again have their beginning. He who is baptized into Christ is united in one corporeity with Him.... In primitive Christianity baptism guaranteed the forgiveness of sins and allegiance to the coming Messiah *(The Mysticism of St. Paul, p.* 19).

For Schweitzer, biblical baptism is the *act of initiation,* not so much into the church universal, and certainly not into a particular denomination, but into our new relationship with Christ. Again, baptism in and of itself does not initiate our new relationship with Christ, like some secret password that unlocks a door, but rather God who has drawn us to that loving response.

How Did Jesus Regard Baptism?

When we look at Jesus' own baptism, we can only shake our heads in wonder, as did John the Baptist.

> Then Jesus came from Galilee to the Jordan to be
> baptized by John. But John tried to deter him, saying, "I
> need to be baptized by you, and do you come to me?"
>   Jesus replied, "Let it be so now; *it is proper for us to
> do this to fulfill all righteousness.*" Then John consented.
>   As soon as Jesus was baptized, he went up out of
> the water (Matthew 3:13-16).

For what possible reason should the sinless Son of God
be baptized? It could have nothing to do with salvation.
The words, "to fulfill all righteousness," sound much
more like obedience or perhaps faithfulness. But because
the sinless Savior is an exception to an otherwise sinful
humanity, His example does not fully explain our own
baptism. At this point, we need to learn what Jesus
taught about baptism for the rest of us.

Jesus' first reference to baptism, as we have already
seen, came during His conversation with Nicodemus.
Jesus obviously placed a high premium on the act of baptism, for He said that unless a person is born of water
and the Spirit he cannot "enter the kingdom of God."
Remember that, immediately after making that statement, Jesus and His disciples went into the Judean
countryside, baptizing those who believed.

But, because Jesus had not yet died for their sins and
because the Holy Spirit had not yet been given to those
who were baptized, the baptism of Jesus appears to be
similar in nature to the baptism of John. Therefore, in
explaining to Nicodemus the role of water in one's spiritual regeneration, Jesus may be making reference to a
later, more clearly-defined, Christian baptism. If so,
Jesus indicates that Christian baptism is the only way to
enter the kingdom of Christ. Strong language, indeed!

For those who accept the traditional ending of Mark's
Gospel (which the two most reliable early manuscripts
do not include), Jesus' tie between faith, baptism, and
salvation would be resoundingly clear: "Whoever believes *and* is baptized will be saved . . ." (Mark 16:16). It

would be much the same as if someone were to say: "Whoever shows up at the Trevi Fountain in Rome on July first and jumps into the fountain will receive a million dollars." Showing up and jumping in would be acts of faith in response to a generous (and unmerited) offer. On the other hand, if someone showed up but did not jump in, we would not expect him to get the million dollars. In the same way, *both* faith *and* baptism are important to salvation. Simply put, from the human standpoint, faith *plus* baptism equals salvation!

Even if one were to dispense with the traditional ending of Mark's Gospel, Matthew's Gospel captures essentially the same message in Jesus' commission to His apostles: "Therefore go and make disciples of all nations, *baptizing them* in the name of the Father and of the Son and of the Holy Spirit . . . " (Matthew 28:19). Discipling and baptizing were two sides of the same coin. Note here how faith itself is silently assumed, and the faith-act of baptism is specifically emphasized. From Jesus' own lips, Christian conversion and baptism are tied together like love and marriage, horse and carriage. As Jesus himself is indicating, you can't properly have one without the other.

Does Baptism Save Us?

Taking the Scriptures in chronological order, the next reference to baptism is in Peter's sermon on the day of Pentecost. Once again, startling language is attached to the act of baptism— this time in conjunction with the element of repentance:

> Peter replied, "Repent and be baptized, every one of you, in the name of Jesus Christ for the forgiveness of your sins(Acts 2:38). [The initial NIV rendering (1973) was: "Repent and be baptized, every one of you, in the name of Jesus Christ *so that your sins may be forgiven.*"]

This passage is so decisive regarding the importance of baptism that it has received careful scrutiny by scholars of all viewpoints. Some traditions have translated the word *for* as "because of," giving support for the position that one is saved on the basis of his repentance and then is baptized as an outward sign of that salvation —*because* he has been saved. However, a consistent rendering of the passage would mean that a person is both being baptized *and repenting* "because of" his salvation. Such an interpretation leaves us with the conclusion that God saves people before they turn their lives to Him through repentance, a scenario that Scripture resoundingly repudiates.

The clear meaning of the passage is that both repentance and baptism lead to one's salvation. Baptism, Peter says, is directly related to our sins' being forgiven. Now there's a thought no one should dismiss lightly: baptism in conjunction with repentance actually initiates the forgiveness of our sins!

Does this mean that in the absence of baptism, our sins are *not* forgiven? And does it further mean that our salvation is not complete until we have actually been baptized? The response of those who heard Peter's words that day shows that baptism is a matter of urgency, because Luke says, "Those who accepted his message were baptized . . ." that very day (Acts 2:41). You don't get the idea that immediate baptism for them was unassociated with their initial question about their spiritual condition.

"What shall we do to get right with God?" they asked. "Repent and be baptized," was Peter's response. Already "cut to the heart" and now open to God's leading, they responded in baptism. Would they have evidenced penitent hearts if they had *refused* baptism?

We've seen previously that Paul re-baptized twelve men from Ephesus because they had submitted only to John's baptism and had not, therefore, received the Holy Spirit. Does this mean that without baptism into Christ, one does not receive the Holy Spirit? The response to Paul's words by those twelve men (Acts 19:5) shows that baptism is crucial, because Luke tells us, "On hearing this, they were baptized into the name of the Lord Jesus." (The special manifestation of the Spirit *prior* to Cornelius's baptism was clearly an exception to the norm, in order to convince Peter that Gentiles, as well as Jews, were eligible for Christian baptism.)

Peter's Understanding of Baptism

Because most of the writing about Christian baptism comes from the apostle Paul, one would hope to find it discussed by other New Testament writers, lest too much be read into some particular emphasis of Paul's. Fortunately, we have the benefit of Peter's inspired writing as well. Peter makes one of the most compelling statements ever about baptism. By comparing the floodwaters that saved Noah to the water of baptism, Peter says bluntly that baptism saves us!

> God waited patiently in the days of Noah while the ark was being built. In it only a few people, eight in all, were saved through water, and this water symbolizes baptism *that now saves you also* — not the removal of dirt from the body but the pledge of a good conscience toward God (1 Peter 3:20, 21).

No mention here of faith, repentance, or confession. Just baptism. And it saves us! But, of course, Peter follows that statement with this one: "It [baptism] saves you by the resurrection of Jesus Christ...."

Peter reminds us that, whatever else might be intrinsic in baptism, it is a symbolic participation in Christ's death, burial, and resurrection. And for good reason. Only in being united with Christ, by the power and in the likeness of His resurrection, can we experience newness of life. So let no one boast of self salvation through the act of baptism! It is the *resurrected Lord* who unites us with himself as we pledge our hearts and our minds to Him!

Furthermore, Peter's omission of the words *faith* or *belief* does not mean that the element of faith is not part of the act of baptism. Jesus himself joined baptism and belief in His great commission to the apostles.

Peter's use of Noah as an illustration drives the point home. Although it may have been the floodwaters that buoyed up the ark and saved those who were inside, Noah and his family would not even have been in the ark had they not believed God's warning about the flood. In fact, without Noah's faith, there would not have been an ark! Noah's outrageous act of building such a vessel demonstrated more faith than most of us are ever called upon to exhibit in our own lives.

Does Faith Take a Back Seat to Baptism?

So what is it that saves us—faith or baptism? The most surprising answer is *neither!* Paul said flatly, *"For it is by grace you have* been saved, through faith—and this not from yourselves, *it is the gift of God*—not by works, so that no one can boast"* (Ephesians 2:8, 9). Neither our mental act of faith nor our participation in baptism, nor both together, could ever save us.

When we pair off faith and baptism and ask which of the two really saves us, we are looking solely at our human response to God. Only if that is absolutely clear can we once again ask the question: from our own human standpoint, is it faith or is it baptism that saves?

We feel comfortable saying that baptism without faith is useless. We realize that merely going through the motions would be perpetrating a fraud. However, we are not equally comfortable saying that faith without baptism is useless. In fact, many fellowships teach that we are saved by faith alone. But, having identified both faith and baptism, as well as repentance and confession, as significant elements of the conversion experience, it is difficult to conclude that faith alone is sufficient for salvation.

Although James was not directly referring to baptism, his letter may help us resolve the apparent conflict:

> What good is it, my brothers, if a man claims to have faith but has no deeds? *Can such faith save him?* Suppose a brother or sister is without clothes and daily food. If one of you says to him, "Go, I wish you well; keep warm and well fed," but does nothing about his physical needs, what good is it? In the same way, *faith by itself, if it is not accompanied by action, is dead* (James 2:14-17).

Although James undoubtedly is referring to the Christian's daily walk, it is clear that he rejects the notion that we are saved by some abstract faith alone. In the next few verses, James gives three examples to emphasize the point. First, even the demons believe in God, but they are not saved by their faith alone. Second, Abraham was "considered righteous for *what he did* when he offered his son Isaac on the altar"—not for his faith alone. And, third, Rahab was "considered righteous for *what she did*" in hiding the spies—not for her faith alone (James 2:19, 21, 25).

One of the clearest pictures of the relationship between faith and faith-responsive action is given to us by Jesus himself. You'll recall the healing of the paralytic, whose friends lowered him on a mat after making an opening in the roof above Jesus by digging through it. "When Jesus *saw* their faith, he said to the paralytic, 'Son, your sins are forgiven'" (Mark 2:5). The faith that prompted forgiveness on this occasion was recognizable, demonstrable. It was not just faith in the heart. For Jesus, faith was perceived through action.

Noah's firm belief that God was sending a flood to destroy the earth would have done him no good had he not acted on it and built the ark. The same is true of us. Even if we have complete faith in Jesus Christ, Peter says that baptism is such strong evidence of our faith that it is as important in God's sight as is our faith itself.

It is the *combination* of faith and baptism that counts. Paul stated the principle that joins faith and baptism into a comprehensive response to God's grace:

> In him you were also circumcised, in the putting off
> of the sinful nature . . . having been buried with him in
> *baptism* and raised with him through your *faith* in the
> power of God, who raised him from the dead
> (Colossians 2:11, 12).

From the *human* perspective, faith expressed in baptism is the combination that saves us. Attempting to separate the two components is the same as asking, "What makes a car go—the motor or the gasoline?" Obviously, neither will work without the other. In fact, there are other necessary parts as well, such as the transmission, the drive shaft, and the tires.

Likewise, there are other elements in the conversion process that also "save" us. We have tentatively included the element of confession, but Paul states a strong case for its role:

> If you confess with your mouth, "Jesus is Lord," and
> believe in your heart that God raised him from the
> dead, you will be saved. For it is with your heart that
> you believe and are justified, and *it is with your mouth
> that you confess and are saved* (Romans 10:9, 10).

So there we have it: we are saved by faith; we are saved by confession; we are saved by baptism. And, from other passages, it appears that repentance is equally indispensable. Are you sufficiently confused?

Perhaps our problem is that we want to play favorites. Those fellowships emphasizing faith naturally focus on Ephesians 2:8 and, not surprisingly, diminish or wholly reject baptism as being essential to salvation. Those fellowships emphasizing baptism naturally focus on 1 Peter 3:21 and, not surprisingly, diminish or wholly reject salvation by faith. And so it goes.

A close friend of mine has focused so intently on such passages as John 3:16 ("whoever *believes* in him shall . . . have eternal life) and Ephesians 1:13 ("Having *believed,* you were marked in him with a seal, the promised Holy

Spirit") that he rules out any possibility that baptism could be tied to salvation. "If baptism is so important to salvation," he asks, "why isn't it included in these passages?" Of course, his focus is altogether understandable, since such passages, standing alone, make no mention of baptism. His problem, however, is in failing to take *all* the passages relating to salvation and to consider them as a whole. Using his selective analysis, one could just as easily conclude from 1 Peter 3:21 (which never mentions faith) that baptism alone saves us.

In our previous example of the million dollars promised to anyone who would show up at the Trevi Fountain and jump in, the person making the offer might say: "If you'll only believe me, you'll get your million dollars." (Compare John 3:16.) It doesn't mean that someone would get the money just for changing his mind and believing, without going to Rome and jumping into the fountain. The intent of the statement is not to substitute faith for action, but to encourage the kind of faith upon which one would be willing to act.

And it would not be surprising to hear the one who offered the money say to a dripping, jubilant Trevi jumper, "Since you believed me, here is your million dollars." (Compare Ephesians 1:13.) Yet those words would never have been spoken if the man had not jumped into the fountain. Faith and belief are rarely viewed in a vacuum apart from the acts they are intended to motivate. Just because a statement about belief does not also mention baptism is no reason to assume baptism is not an essential response to that belief—especially when other passages tie them directly together.

To use the wedding analogy, someone might say to a couple: "You know, you two really ought to be married. You're a great couple." Would omitting any reference to the wedding ceremony suggest a belief that the ceremony is unessential to the initiation of their marriage or to the benefits that would attach?

If it is possible to get overly technical about baptism—and it is—it is also possible to get overly technical about references to faith that are lifted at random and do not provide the complete picture. Relying upon only a few selected verses of Scripture—even when they appear on their face to be straightforward and unambiguous—can mislead us and distort our understanding.

Working Our Way to Heaven Won't Work

Some fear that viewing baptism as essential for salvation will make it a "work" of man, replacing the grace of God. While baptism is an affirmative physical act done by man in response to God, it cannot fairly be called a "work" (at least with the connotation of earned salvation) any more than the affirmative mental act of faith that one might make.

If baptism is a work, so is faith. In fact, the word *work* is never used in connection with baptism, but is used pointedly in reference to faith. Remember what the crowd from Capernaum asked Jesus? "What must we do to do the works God requires?" Jesus answered, "The work of God is this: to believe in the one he has sent" (John 6:28, 29).

Both faith and baptism are human responses to God's initiative. Both are acts of free will. In neither baptism nor faith are we mindless puppets or robots. We *choose* to be baptized, yes. But we also *choose* to believe. And unless we choose to respond affirmatively to God's grace, we cannot receive His salvation.

The popular idea of salvation by *faith alon* is wrong in two critical ways. From the human standpoint, the acts of repentance, confession, and baptism are as significant in the conversion process as is the act of faith. From God's perspective, salvation is by *grace* alone, not faith alone. When we accept the offer of His grace, God saves us (or justifies us, or regenerates us) through grace *plus nothing*.

If we're concerned that baptism requires us to *do* something in order to receive salvation, we should be equally concerned that faith also requires us to *do* something.

To anyone who thinks we could ever do anything that would merit salvation—whether it be believing or being baptized—Paul's words bear repeating: "For it is by grace you have been saved, through faith—and this not from yourselves, it is the gift of God—*not by works,* so that no one can boast" (Ephesians 2:8, 9).

Far from baptism's being a "work" we can perform and thereby achieve salvation, baptism is perhaps the sublime statement that we are *not* relying on our own moral goodness to win the day. The very act of being immersed in a pool of water demonstrates that we are depending on Christ for our salvation—not our own merits. Who in the world would have conceived of such a patently peculiar act if the goal were to *work* our way to Heaven! The humiliating act of being plunged beneath water is ennobled only by the fact that baptism is an appointed trysting place with God. Like Jesus' washing of the disciples' feet, baptism is a demonstration of self-effacing love.

Having grown up in a fellowship that seems at times to "overwork" the true significance of baptism, I am sympathetic with those who resist being caught in the same trap. However, fearing that baptism is a "work" of man that negates the saving grace of God misses the point. If baptism is a "work," then "work" is what Jesus commanded. And it is a "work" in which Jesus himself participated. If it is through "work" that we are promised the gift of the Holy Spirit, then show me how I can do that "work!"

Can you imagine a bride saying that she doesn't really want a wedding after all because she's afraid people might think she was earning her way into a relationship? Just as it would be odd to say that a wedding is a "work," it is difficult to imagine that any of the first Christian converts would have thought they were engaged in "work" at the moment of their baptism. From what they said and did, "work" was the farthest thing from their minds.

Their rejoicing is not the attitude of someone who is still on the job. Their rejoicing is more characteristic of the person celebrating his first day of vacation away from work. In the case of the Jewish Christians, it meant freedom from the works of the law that had so burdened them. For New Testament Christians, baptism was the joyful celebration of a bride who had just experienced the ultimate expression of her love.

It has occurred to me recently that there is a rather grand irony in the belief that, since baptism is a "work" of man, it ought to be completely separated from the initiation of one's salvation. When baptism is divorced altogether from forgiveness and justification, its observance becomes simply a legal requirement to be complied with because Christ told us to do it. As a lawyer, I cringe at the thought of making baptism no more than an after-the-fact legal technicality.

Whatever else it may be, baptism is an occasion of covenanting with God. It is as different from a legal technicality as the wedding ceremony is from the minister's signing of the wedding certificate after the bride and groom have left for their honeymoon. Baptism is not a perfunctory signing of the certificate because the law requires it. Baptism is the divine wedding ceremony itself through which the Holy Spirit seals the covenant we have chosen in faith to enter.

If anyone is concerned about baptism's being a "work," then let us drop the notion that baptism is an afterthought to salvation. That notion only minimizes and trivializes what was intended to be a loving act of sublime worship—not an obligatory act of mandated obedience. When baptism is joined with salvation, it is tied with grace; when baptism is joined with obedience, it is tied with works. If we want to keep baptism from being a "work," then we must honor it as God's pathway to covenant salvation—not a legalistic hurdle the new convert is asked to jump simply for the sake of jumping.

Like most Christians, when I think of God's grace, I *want* to believe that it acts wholly apart from anything I might do. I want to be in the position of one who is *completely passive* in the matter because I know how hopeless it would be ever to attempt to earn it or deserve it.

But if that were the way God's grace were dispensed, it would have to be *dispensed*—not simply be made available—to believers and unbelievers alike. Were grace to be bestowed in the face of total passivity, no one justly could be left out. And while I am not eager that anyone be "left out," the Scriptures plainly teach that not all will acknowledge Jesus Christ as Lord.

We must see God's grace as a rope let down into the pit of our human sinfulness. But for God's grace, we would not have any means of rescue. Yet if we want to be saved from our doomed condition, we must take hold of the rope so that God can pull us up. The act of faith-responsive baptism is one of the ways in which we "take hold" of God's mercy. While there is not a chance in the world that we could ever pull ourselves up out of our sinful condition, neither can we expect God's grace to be effective while we remain completely passive.

The Lesson from Naaman

There was once a man who thought God was only concerned with basics, not details. He believed that God cared only about the essence of a matter and would not require strict obedience by man. For him, externals had little, if anything, to do with pleasing God. You probably remember the story of Naaman, a high-ranking commander in the army of Aram (Syria), who was afflicted by leprosy. At the suggestion of his wife's servant, Naaman went to the prophet Elisha to be healed:

> So Naaman went with his horses and chariots and stopped at the door of Elisha's house. Elisha sent a

messenger to say to him, "Go, wash yourself seven times in the Jordan, and your flesh will be restored and you will be cleansed."

But Naaman went away angry and said, "I thought that he would surely come out to me and stand and call on the name of the Lord his God, wave his hand over the spot and cure me of my leprosy. Are not Abana and Pharpar, the rivers of Damascus, better than any of the waters of Israel? Couldn't I wash in them and be cleansed?" So he turned and went off in a rage.

Naaman's servants went to him and said, "My father, *if the prophet had told you to do some great thing, would you not have done it? How much more, then, when he tells you, 'wash and be cleansed'!"*

So he went down and dipped himself in the Jordan seven times, as the man of God had told him, and his flesh was restored and became clean like that of a young boy (2 Kings 5:9-14).

The servant's advice is altogether sensible even today. If God were to tell us to do some great thing, wouldn't our faith lead us to attempt it? How much more readily, then, ought we to obey when He gives this simple command: "Repent and be baptized for the forgiveness of your sins!"

Reflections

1. At what point does a couple's committed love relationship become recognizable as a marriage?

2. At what point does the human response to God's grace bring one into a right relationship with God?

3. What saves us: faith, repentance, baptism, or grace?

4. What was Jesus trying to tell us through his own baptism?

5. In what way is faith a "work"?

6. How did you perceive your own baptism in terms of being a "work"?

7. When baptism is required as an act of obedience *following* salvation, can it rise above being a type of legal technicality?

8. If baptism is viewed only as an outward sign of one's faith, does it reflect the answer Peter gave on Pentecost (Acts 2:38) to those who wanted to know what they should do to be saved?

9. What lesson is to be learned from the experience of Naaman?

10. Can baptism "for the remission of sin" ever be practiced legalistically?

CHAPTER 5

HOW ESSENTIAL IS THE CEREMONY?

"Without baptism, faith is like a disembodied soul.

G. R. Beasley-Murray

If baptism is important, is it also *essential?* How are we to respond to the millions of people in the world who have never been baptized but who nevertheless call themselves Christians? Are they brothers and sisters in Christ? Do they have the hope of Heaven?

None of the elements of conversion, whether faith or baptism or repentance or confession, fully explains salvation. When, as we saw earlier, Peter tells us we are saved through baptism, he is referring to the human side of the conversion process. From our standpoint, baptism is our pledge of a good conscience toward God. But the writer of Hebrews urgently calls our attention to *Christ's* role in our salvation.

After explaining the interrelationship between external ritual and the internal cleansing of the conscience, the writer stresses the point that no external ritual— including baptism—would be sufficient but for the sacrifice of Jesus Christ on the cross. The ritual acts of worship under the law of Moses illustrate the superiority of Christ's sacrifice on the cross:

> [Worship in the earthly tabernacle] is an illustration for the present time, indicating that the gifts and sacrifices being offered *were not able to clear the conscience of the worshiper*. They are only a matter of food and drink and *various ceremonial washings*—external regulations applying until the time of the new order (Hebrews 9:9, 10).

> The blood of goats and bulls and the ashes of a heifer sprinkled on those who are ceremonially unclean sanctify them so that they are outwardly clean. *How much more, then, will the blood of Christ . . . cleanse our consciences* from acts that lead to death, so that we may serve the living God! (Hebrews 9:13, 14).

> Therefore, brothers, since we have confidence to enter the Most Holy Place by the blood of Jesus, by a new and living way opened for us through the curtain, that is, his body, and since we have a great priest over the house of God, let us draw near to God with a sincere heart in full assurance of faith, *having our hearts sprinkled to cleanse us from a guilty conscience and having our bodies washed with pure water* (Hebrews 10:19-22).

When the believer's body is washed in the water of baptism, the blood of Christ is the real cleansing agent. Does that sound strange? Normally, we do not think of blood as being a cleansing agent, but rather as a stain requiring cleansing.

And who could bear the thought of immersing one's self in a bath of blood? But just as a washing in blood would not cleanse the outer body, a washing in water does not itself cleanse the inner conscience.

Baptism "saves" us, not because of the external ritual of washing in water (what *we* do), but because the act of faith puts us into contact with the saving blood of Christ (what *He* has already done). Baptism testifies to our consciences' being cleansed, forgiven, and freed from guilt by the sacrifice of Jesus Christ and the regeneration that comes from the Spirit.

Karl Barth listed many ways in which baptism is essential:

> One ought to and must say of [baptism] in the words of Scripture: it saves, sanctifies, purifies, mediates, and gives the forgiveness of sins and the grace of the Holy Spirit; it effects the new birth *(The Teaching of the Church Regarding Baptism,* pp. 9, 29).

Although Karl Barth's view of baptism might at first resemble "baptismal regeneration," he opposed the practice of infant baptism precisely for the reason that faith is missing in the baptized infant. Therefore, Barth would not deny the crucial importance of faith in the conversion process. Nor would Barth have overlooked the central role of the Holy Spirit in planting us and engrafting us into the Lord Jesus Christ. He correctly appeals to "the words of Scripture" in pointing out the many ways in which baptism is indispensable to the conversion process as God asks us to participate in that process.

What Is the Essence of Baptism?

Let's return to our analogy with marriage. What makes a marriage? The love? The relationship? The commitment? The vows? Is it the minister's words pronouncing the couple to be husband and wife? Or perhaps the completed paperwork, signed and mailed to the court clerk? Would anyone suggest that the marriage is not valid until actually consummated by intimate physical relations? (Among some tribes in Papua New Guinea, no marriage is recognized until children are born!)

Are we being overly analytical? Certainly *all* of these factors combine to make the marriage. Even aside from the necessary compliance with civil authority, a number of identifiable elements must come together in order to constitute a marriage.

But if you were *forced* to choose, which would be the most important factor in a marriage? Would it be the committed love relationship or the wedding ceremony? Most people would choose the committed love relationship. And the same is true in the conversion process. If forced to choose, we would say that the more important factor is our commitment of faith to Christ, not the wedding ceremony of baptism.

Without at least a pretension of faith, there would rarely be a personally-chosen baptism at all. That is why it makes sense for Jesus to have said, "Whoever believes and is baptized will be saved, but whoever does not believe will be condemned" (Mark 16:16), without referring a second time to baptism. If a person doesn't believe, it isn't necessary to add the superfluous words, "and is not baptized."

The prerequisite nature of faith is also undoubtedly the reason Jesus linked condemnation with unbelief—without any mention of baptism—when explaining salvation to Nicodemus: "Whoever believes in him is not condemned, but whoever does not believe stands condemned already ... " (John 3:18). Without faith, we don't even reach the point of faith-responsive baptism.

The heart, soul, and essence of baptism is not the act of going under the water. Peter said, "[It's] not the removal of dirt from the body but the pledge of a good conscience toward God" (1 Peter 3:21). If there were no change of heart, no faith in God's promises, and no commitment to Christ's lordship, one could go through the wedding ceremony of baptism every day of the year, every year of his life, and never have a proper relationship with God.

What Paul said about the relationship between circumcision and being a Jew could also be said of baptism and being a Christian:

> A man is not a Jew if he is only one outwardly, nor is circumcision merely outward and physical. No, a man is a Jew if he is one inwardly; and circumcision is circumcision of the heart, by the Spirit, not by the written code (Romans 2:28, 29).

Paul just as easily could have said: "A person is not a Christian if he is only one outwardly, nor is baptism merely outward and physical. No, a person is a Christian if he is one inwardly; and baptism is baptism of the heart, by the Spirit, not by the mere act of obedience to the command to be baptized."

It is crucial to have a proper perspective of the essence of baptism and to establish the clear priority of one's faith and his commitment to Christ's lordship. One need only look at the many people who have gone through the motions of baptism without knowing why, or without truly committing themselves to the relationship that they ought to have with Christ. The world is filled to the point of disgrace with "Christians" for whom Christ in their lives is not important. It reminds one of the thousands of marriages that have failed despite luxurious weddings and volumes of spoken vows.

Can Baptism Be Spiritualized Away?

If baptism without a personal relationship with Christ is of serious concern—and it is—the way we too often have raced to the opposite extreme of relationship without baptism is of equal concern. A number of fellowships within the Christian community no longer see baptism as important to forgiveness, salvation, or even body identity. For them, subjective feelings about a relationship have completely replaced ceremony. They zealously urge that a faith relationship with Christ is needed for conversion, but perhaps never encourage the believer to be baptized. Salvation is received the moment one "accepts Jesus Christ into his heart as his personal Lord and Savior," and baptism—whether then or later—is often completely ignored.

Typical of this approach is the prayer a well-known evangelist invites his crusade and television audiences to pray in order to become Christians: "O God, I know that I am a sinner and need Your forgiveness. I believe that You died for my sins. I want to turn from my sins. I now invite You to come into my heart and life. I want to trust You as Savior and follow You as Lord, in the fellowship of Your church. In Christ's name, amen." Without any mention of baptism, the evangelist assures those who pray the prayer that God has forgiven them and adopted them into His family. If baptism plays any role at all in the life of the believer, it never comes across in the media broadcasts or in his best-selling books.

Taking such a believe-and-receive position requires interpreting figuratively the many Biblical references to baptism, as if baptism were only a spiritual experience—completely unassociated with water. And, frankly, there are some passages that lend themselves to such an interpretation. In the letter to Titus, for example, it is less than clear whether Paul is referring to a literal, or merely a figurative, washing:

> But when the kindness and love of God our Savior appeared, he saved us, not because of righteous things we had done, but because of his mercy. He saved us through the washing of rebirth and renewal by the Holy Spirit, whom he poured out on us generously through Jesus Christ our Savior, so that, having been justified by his grace, we might become heirs having the hope of eternal life (Titus 3:4-7).

Still, we cannot deny Jesus' command to teach and baptize the nations, or overlook the frequent references to water baptism, or ignore the specific individual examples of New Testament converts. Some of them were told to believe, others to repent, still others to confess, but all, without exception, were baptized—in water—as part of their conversion experience.

The Many Examples of Water Baptism

A review of all the specific instances of conversion in the New Testament is revealing. The list begins with the multitude on Pentecost who had been told to repent and be baptized. *"Those who accepted his message were baptized,* and about three thousand were added to their number that day"* (Acts 2:41).

The Samaritans responded to the gospel message through belief and baptism:

> But when they believed Philip as he preached the good news of the kingdom of God and the name of Jesus Christ, *they were baptized*, both men and women. Simon himself believed and was baptized (Acts 8:12, 13).

The Ethiopian eunuch did not entertain the idea that baptism was just so much figurative spiritualizing about the change that was, at that very moment, taking place in his life:

> As they traveled along the road, they came to some water and the eunuch said, "Look, here is water. Why shouldn't I be baptized?" And he gave orders to stop the chariot. *Then both Philip and the eunuch went down into the water and Philip baptized him* (Acts 8:36-38).

Saul had a more dramatic conversion experience than any of us will ever know, yet he, too, was baptized: *"He got up and was baptized,* and after taking some food, he regained his strength"* (Acts 9:18, 19).

Cornelius had already been baptized with the Holy Spirit, yet Peter commanded that Cornelius be baptized with water:

> Then Peter said, "Can anyone keep these people from being baptized *with water*? They have received the Holy Spirit just as we have." *So he ordered that they be baptized* in the name of Jesus Christ (Acts 10:46-48).

In the city of Philippi, Lydia's baptism came in response to her openness to receive the message being preached: "The Lord opened her heart to respond to Paul's message. *When she and the members of her household were baptized,* she invited us to her home" (Acts 16:14, 15).

We have seen how baptism was part of the Philippian jailer's conversion: "At that hour of the night the jailer took them and washed their wounds; *then immediately he and all his family were baptized*" (Acts 16:33).

In the city of Corinth, on Paul's second missionary journey, Crispus and many other Corinthians were baptized: "Crispus, the synagogue ruler, and his entire household believed in the Lord; and many of the Corinthians who heard him *believed and were baptized*" (Acts 18:8). Paul reflects on those baptisms when writing his first letter to the Corinthians (1 Corinthians 1:14-16):

> I am thankful that I did not baptize any of you except Crispus and Gaius, so no one can say that you were baptized into my name. (Yes, I also baptized the household of Stephanas; beyond that, I don't remember if I baptized anyone else.)

Paul's recollection about having baptized Crispus also removes a question that might be raised in those few passages (for example, Acts 4:4; 5:14; and 9:42) which record that groups of people believed and became followers of Christ, yet do not mention their baptisms. Without Paul's mention of Crispus, we might conclude from Luke's account that Crispus believed, but was not baptized (Acts 18:8). But Paul clearly says that he was. In this detail, we can see that the New Testament writers assumed responsive baptism when referring to obedient faith.

In the face of these specific examples of New Testament conversion, why would anyone consider the act of baptism to be nothing more than a "spiritual" washing? There's simply too much water involved to reach that conclusion. Does this mean that the New Testament teaches baptismal regeneration or (Heaven forbid!) water regeneration in which the mere act of baptism equates with sanctification?

Does the Bible teach sacramental salvation? Obviously not. But neither does it limit baptism to a mystical spiritual regeneration.

Are We Just "Living Together" With Christ?

Returning to the comparison with marriage may be helpful. What Christian would spiritualize the marriage ceremony so as to eliminate any need of it? Are we ready to say that the relationship is all there is—that as long as a man and a woman love each other and live together in a state of commitment, they have God's approval?

While no reasonable person would say that the wedding ceremony is the essence of the marriage, surely Christians have not joined the world in accepting unwedded bliss. And if we cringe at the thought that simply living together would be acceptable in God's sight, why aren't we concerned that there are believers who have never participated in the wedding ceremony of baptism? They may be "living together" with Christ, but they are not yet completely united with Him.

Of course, the analogy with "living together" is not precisely parallel, because there is nothing immoral about being simply a believer in Christ. In fact, one's faith commitment to Christ is greatly desirable. Nevertheless, the analogy is biblical to the extent that it shows the need for compliance with all of God's commands before receiving the full benefits of the relationship.

And what are those spiritual benefits that the Scriptures attach to baptism? *Forgiveness of sins* (Acts 2:38; 22:16); *a new birth* (John 3:5); *spiritual regeneration* (Titus 3:5); *union with Christ* (Galatians 3:27); *identification with Christ's death, burial, and resurrection* (Romans 6:3-5); *sonship with God the Father* (Galatians 3:26, 27); *membership in the body of Christ* (1 Corinthians 12:13); *belonging to the church* (Acts 2:41); *receiving the gift of the Holy Spirit* (Acts 2:38); and *eternal salvation* (Mark 16:16;1 Peter 3:21).

If the wedding ceremony of baptism brings us formally and fully into covenant relationship with Christ, then, without baptism, we have none of the blessings that are promised as part of the covenant.

And what about our use of the name "Christian"? By what right do we wear Christ's name other than through the wedding ceremony of baptism? Certainly it would be highly unusual if an unmarried woman were to take the name of her fiance prior to the day of the wedding. At the point of accepting Christ's teaching, one may be a disciple of Christ and a believer, but, without baptism, can one rightfully appropriate the name "Christian"? Is it possible that before submitting to baptism, we are adopting Christ's name prematurely?

"But," someone will say, "surely God doesn't operate this way. God is not a God of externals. It's what's in the heart that counts, nothing more." And, of course, there is much truth to those statements. God once gave the nation of Israel temples, tabernacles, priests, and animal sacrifices, but now He calls for worship in which our bodies are tabernacles, we ourselves are priests, and Christ is our sacrifice. For the most part, the external has given way to the internal.

But carrying the logic of substance over form too far would also eliminate the visible, tangible elements of the Lord's Supper. Sadly enough, more and more fellowships appear to be abandoning this Communion as well. It, too, has been spiritualized into rarity, if not oblivion.

We must remember that the same apostles who insisted that the rituals required by the law of Moses were abolished in Christ's kingdom also observed the Lord's Supper and practiced the rite of baptism. Although Christ took away the rituals of Jewish worship, He left us with these two visible reminders of His love and called on us to look beyond them to Him. Does the true believer honor Christ by denying the importance of either of these ceremonies, which Christ himself instituted? Can we ignore either of them with impunity?

The Thief Has Stolen the Show

When discussing baptism, the question about the thief on the cross inevitably arises. "If baptism is essential for salvation," the question goes, "then why is it that Jesus promised salvation to the thief on the cross, even though the thief presumably had never been baptized?"

My first reaction to the thief-on-the-cross argument is to wonder why no one asks about others whose sins Jesus forgave during His ministry (e.g., the sinful woman, Luke 7:47), for whom there is also no record of any baptism, either before or after Jesus' death. Why ignore them and focus instead on the poor thief?

The fact is that they are all in the same spiritual boat. And what they have in common is that their contact with Jesus was before His death (which ushered in the New Covenant), before His resurrection (in the likeness of which one is raised through Christian baptism), before Jesus gave His apostles the Great Commission (whereby baptism was commanded), and before the advent of the Holy Spirit (whose indwelling is promised to all baptized believers).

Frankly, if I were looking for exceptions, I would wonder why we are never told anything about the apostles themselves having been baptized. Were they ever baptized? If so, when? Would it have been when they were baptizing others in Judea? We simply don't know. But because Jesus himself was baptized to fulfill all righteousness, it is difficult to believe that He would never have called upon His closest disciples to follow His own example.

Whatever might have been the case, one thing is certain: none of us is one of the chosen Twelve. What Jesus did or did not require of them is not known. For each of us, the only question can be, "What does He require of me?"

A second observation is that Jesus, as the Son of God, could suspend both natural laws and spiritual laws as the occasion demanded, and often did. Like His Father in Heaven, He had mercy on whom He would have mercy. It was Jesus' divine right to deal with the thief in any way that He chose, without changing any duty we might have. Acts of clemency do not legalize the forgiven conduct. God's desire is for us to be baptized.

A third observation is that the thief was faced with an exceptional physical circumstance that made baptism humanly impossible. Why didn't Jesus command the thief to be baptized? Setting all possible theological speculation aside, the fact is that, at that moment, the thief was nailed to a cross!

God has never asked us to do the impossible, including the hypothetical Africans in the middle of the desert who have no water in which to be baptized. Why not let God worry about exceptional circumstances?

Without presuming to make a judgment that only God can make, we see exceptional results in exceptional situations by once again drawing a parallel with marriage. If an unmarried man and an unmarried woman were to find themselves marooned alone for a lifetime on a desert island, would it be proper for them to live together as husband and wife without the benefit of a wedding ceremony officiated by someone authorized to perform marriages? Most of us would answer yes. If we are right about that, would not the principle of impossibility apply equally to the wedding ceremony of baptism?

The thief on the cross was an exception. Why would anyone want to rest his eternal security on what amounts to loophole theology? There could be no greater loss than letting the thief on the cross rob us of our salvation.

What *we* need to do is be honest with ourselves and with God's Word, and prayerfully consider what God would have us to do about baptism—right now, right where we are—long before we find ourselves on a cross, or in the middle of a desert, or in the emergency room of a hospital.

Reflections

1. In what ways is Christ's sacrificial death superior to the ritual sacrifices of Moses?

2. What does the superiority of Christ's sacrifice imply about the essence of the ritual of baptism?

3. What is the value of a baptism when it is not based on a faith relationship?

4. What is the value of a faith relationship when it is not accompanied by baptism?

5. Is there any example in Scripture of what is popularly known as "the sinner's prayer" whereby one is said to become a Christian solely by accepting Jesus into one's heart?

6. What is the best evidence that biblical baptism is more than a spiritualized encounter with God?

7. What benefits are associated with water baptism in the New Testament?

8. Why do you suppose God would eliminate external Jewish ritual only to require the external rituals of baptism and Communion?

9.   What lessons can we learn regarding baptism from the thief on the cross?

10.   Can a case be made that baptized believers have a stronger faith than non-baptized believers? Is that a legitimate comparison to make in view of Christ's command to baptize the nations?

CHAPTER 6

CAN THE CEREMONY BE DELAYED?

"Baptism and faith are but the outside and the inside of the same thing."

James Denney

Some fellowships see baptism as an important part of the Christian's response to God, but only as an outward symbol of an inward washing by which one's salvation has already been sealed. While they teach that the person who has been saved by faith should submit to baptism as a matter of obedience and faithfulness, they do not see baptism as crucial in any way to salvation. Doctrinally, this position assumes that salvation comes before baptism. Practically, this means that one may be baptized days, weeks, or months following the conversion experience. The sooner the better, perhaps, but the timing is basically a matter of convenience.

This conclusion follows naturally from the belief that baptism is not essential to salvation. Perhaps it is *ultimately* required, as evidence of a willingness to obey Christ's commands, but it is not immediately essential.

By this view, if one were to refuse baptism after his conversion experience, there would be a serious question about the genuineness of his conversion in the first place.

This position is radically different from the conversions of the first Christians. The key word suggested by the scriptural montage of New Testament accounts of conversion is "immediately." The three thousand on Pentecost, for example, were baptized "that day" (Acts 2:47). When told of the good news about Jesus, the Ethiopian eunuch immediately ordered his chariot to stop so he could be baptized. Immediately after the scales fell from Saul's eyes in the home of Ananias, Saul got up and was baptized. Cornelius was baptized immediately after the Holy Spirit's presence indicated God's approval of Gentile baptism. Lydia was baptized immediately after her heart was opened to the gospel message, and, across town, the Philippian jailer was baptized the same hour of the night in which he committed his life to Christ.

Many fellowships today do not have the sense of urgency that was characteristic of baptism among first-century Christians. Instead of baptism's being spontaneous and immediate, today there is often a rather planned formalism about the matter. For example, some churches have special baptismal services in which a number of new believers, converted during the past week or month, will be baptized.

Rarely today is a new convert who accepts Christ as his Savior in the middle of the night baptized "at the same hour." I see a growing trend even in my own fellowship to delay baptism until the church is assembled together for its regular time of public worship.

Which picture does your own baptism more closely resemble? Was it an integral part of your initial conversion to Christ, or was it postponed until a formal occasion or ceremony?

Why the Delay?

In many fellowships, the delay between a person's commitment of faith and subsequent baptism is purposeful on the part of the church. There has long been the feeling that baptism ought to be preceded by a period of religious instruction following one's commitment of faith. Although the origin of such a practice is not altogether clear, it may be an offshoot from the catechism instruction associated with confirmation (where infant baptism is practiced) or with the idea that a person needs to know something about the church he is joining when he is baptized (where baptism is seen as entrance into a particular church).

Whatever might be the reason for the practice of pre-baptismal instruction and the delay it necessitates, it does not have its roots in New Testament Christianity. Whether it was those who were baptized on Pentecost, or the Ethiopian eunuch, or the Philippian jailer, New Testament converts were baptized at the point of their conversion—many after only one sermon! Jesus himself told the apostles to baptize those who became disciples, and *then* to teach them to observe all the things that He had commanded (Matthew 28:19, 20).

Unlike those ministers who commonly require a period of premarital counseling before performing the wedding ceremony, in New Testament baptism, the "premarital counseling" came before one reached the point of faith and then continued after one was baptized into Christ. Pre-baptism instruction was also pre-faith instruction.

The preaching of the gospel led to faith, and baptism immediately followed on the heels of faith. Between an expression of committed faith and faith-responsive baptism, there was no intervening period of instruction. *After* baptism, of course, the early Christians continued in the apostles' teaching as they grew in knowledge and matured in their Christian walk (Acts 2:42).

87

The concern with postponed baptism is not that God would condemn to hell the believer who might die before he is baptized. Rather, the real concern is the implication that flows from the difference in timing between the modern practice and the biblical pattern.

The farther removed baptism is from the point of faith and commitment, the more ritualistic and the less "necessary" it becomes. Baptism that is urgent—immediate—recognizes that baptism is an integral part of the conversion experience. When baptism is easily delayed—postponed—there is an inference that baptism is *not* essential. It is merely a ritualistic ceremony to be observed, important though that ceremony may be.

Those who practice postponed baptism are missing the point. Think back on what we have already seen. Are we saved through faith? Absolutely. Is salvation a matter of grace? Over and over again the apostle Paul has driven home that fact. But from all the scriptures we have reviewed thus far, the covenant role of baptism simply cannot be ignored.

We must ask ourselves: has baptism no role in one's entrance into the kingdom? No role in the forgiveness of sins? No role whatsoever in being saved? Need we review once again the passages that teach so plainly that, *from the human standpoint,* baptism does in fact play a vital part in salvation, forgiveness, and entry into the kingdom? In fact, the New Testament pattern of baptisms emphasizes that baptism is not only a *vital* point in the conversion process, but the *focal* point.

It is easy to overlook the fact that on the day of Pentecost (Acts 2), it was those who were *already believers* who asked, in effect, "What *more* must we do to have our sins forgiven?" Why ask such a question unless you have already believed, been convicted of sin, and turned your heart to God for His solution? They wanted to know how God desired them to act on their faith. In response to their faith-motivated question, Peter told them what more they needed to do before receiving salvation.

This point cannot be overemphasized. It was to those who were already *believers* that Peter responded, in effect, "Those of you who have believed the gospel we have preached today need to respond to God's divine initiative by committing yourselves to a changed life (repentance) and by making a public demonstration of your faith in Christ (baptism) so that (through your faith that prompts these external, visible actions) you may be forgiven of your sins." And Peter might well have added: ". . . by the merciful love that God has already shown you in Christ Jesus, which none of us could ever merit through anything we might ever do."

Our analogy to marriage may once again be helpful. Suppose we were to treat baptism as a ceremony that can be postponed at one's convenience on the rationale that, after all, it is the faith relationship itself that really counts. Would we be satisfied with the parallel conclusion that as long as a man and a woman are truly committed to each other for life, they can go ahead and live together until the wedding ceremony actually takes place?

We are probably on safe ground to say that few, if any, who believe in postponed baptism would approve of a couple's living together before marriage, even for the shortest period of time. They realize that marriage is not legitimate until the wedding itself takes place. Neither the responsibilities nor the benefits of a marriage are vested until the couple is pronounced "husband" and "wife." Their union of body and spirit has no sanction before that time, and should children be born prior to the wedding, they would be considered illegitimate.

All this seems clear enough with regard to marriage, but somehow we attach less importance to the more important wedding ceremony of baptism, in which our lives are joined together with Christ. Just as the wedding ceremony is the *actualization* of the marriage, not simply the *confirmation,* the same is true of baptism. Baptism is not just sentimental symbolism. Baptism *achieves* something. God works *"through"* baptism and "by" baptism to bring about our new relationship with Him. Baptism is the Holy Spirit's *instrument* of conversion, not simply our witness to that conversion. Until baptism occurs, our conversion experience is incomplete.

A Case of Bad Timing

Those who justify baptism as merely an outward sign of a salvation already inwardly received, may want to consider what might have happened if history had been altered only slightly with the thief on the cross. If Pilate had issued a last-minute reprieve and ordered that the thief be set free from the cross, would the thief then have been subject to baptism? Suppose it happened after Pentecost and the advent of the Holy Spirit. Would the thief have been asked to submit to baptism as a matter of obedience, or perhaps as an outward sign of an inward grace? And what if he had refused, saying he was saved at the moment he accepted Christ? Would his salvation thereby have been jeopardized?

These questions point out that the complete separation of salvation and baptism raises thorny problems that are avoided when baptism is seen as an integral part of the conversion experience. It's not simply a matter of achieving theological neatness. Putting salvation before baptism confers the ultimate spiritual privilege of salvation before satisfaction of one of the human-responsive elements said by Scripture to be essential prior to that salvation.

Church Practice a Test of Doctrine

The most serious problem with baptism and its timing in the process of one's turning to God is that church practice inevitably exposes Scriptural understanding. If a church's *practice* is different from the practice of the church in the New Testament, it is likely that its *doctrine* is also different from first-century Christianity. If the *timing* of baptism today is different from the *timing* of baptism as seen in the lives of New Testament converts, it is likely that the *doctrine* of baptism is somehow skewed. Or, to put it another way: if we believe our understanding of baptism's role is the same as the apostles' understanding, why does their practice of baptism *look* different from ours? The timing of one's baptism may not be as insignificant as we may have felt. There's a sense in which doing Bible things *in Bible ways* keeps us out of trouble.

Is Bad Timing Fatal?

When baptism is separated from the conversion process, the *timing* is simply wrong. But is that timing really of great significance to God? When it comes to the matter of weddings and living together and having babies, we tend to place a lot of importance on timing. Why then would we think that the timing of one's baptism is any less significant? Just how serious is it when one misunderstands the timing of baptism? Is that person without hope?

In legal matters, it sometimes happens that several essential conditions must occur in order for a transaction to take place. When all of the conditions have been met, the transaction has legal validity. If one of the essential conditions is overlooked, it results in failure of the transaction. Not all of the conditions have been fully met.

But where the parties are unaware of the unsatisfied condition, they may believe that they have engaged in a valid transaction and proceed to act upon that mistaken assumption. Are they headed for trouble somewhere down the road? Not necessarily. If the essential condition is subsequently satisfied, the transaction becomes legally valid—after the fact.

The point is this. Although at a given time the parties were wrong about the validity of the transaction, when the final essential condition was eventually met, the circumstances turned out to be what the two parties had thought (incorrectly) to be true all along.

The application of this principle is simple enough. There are those who believe that, simply on the basis of their faith in Christ, they are Christians before they are baptized. Yet, because God desires baptism to be a part of the divine process of salvation, an essential condition on their part has not yet been met. Is all necessarily lost? When those believers respond in faith to be baptized, then it could be possible that all of the conditions have finally and decisively been met. If the legal analogy holds in God's eyes, the human response is now complete. God's free gift of salvation will have been properly accepted.

If a person was not fully in Christ when he thought he was, he may *become* a fully-obedient person in Christ at the point of joining his Lord in baptism. Even though his baptism follows his initial commitment of faith by a time greater than would be accorded by New Testament practice, his obedience in the act of baptism may at last complete the package of essential faith-action elements required for true conversion. The delayed ceremony of baptism relates back to the faith that prompted it and completes his loving response to God.

Of course, our relationship with God is not a legal transaction, because there is nothing we could exchange with God that would be worthy consideration for the gift He has given us. Neither our compliance with a single condition, nor even a whole package of conditions—even with the "right timing"—could ever be sufficient to satisfy what is essentially a unilateral transaction.

Should we feel comfortable resorting to the kind of legalistic formularizing warned against in chapter one— particularly since there is no direct scriptural authority that verifies the conclusion? The process of turning to God and becoming a Christian is not a matter of legal technicalities and magic formulas. It is a matter of becoming involved in a dynamic relationship between ourselves and a loving God. Hence, the picture of a wedding ceremony rather than a court trial.

"But," someone will ask, "suppose a person dies after coming to believe in Christ but before the time he is to be baptized. Does that mean he would not be saved?" As with every other question dealing with man's salvation, only the God of all Judgment can answer that for us. I would be neither surprised nor disappointed if God were to save in this situation. God is a merciful God. But what *God* may or may not do in that situation doesn't give us room to make baptism anything less than what Christ intended it to be—an essential part of our response to His divine initiative.

If you are uncomfortable in using this "relation-back" approach to link up a subsequent baptism with a previous commitment of faith (I've been there myself), this thought may help: where a person who has believed in Christ over a period of many years learns for the first time the importance of baptism as part of his response to God, do we deny him baptism because he wasn't immediately baptized when he first turned to God in faith?

Or, more importantly, do we ask him to somehow *undo* his faith and start from the beginning as if he were an unbeliever? Of course not. We gladly receive his confession of faith and rejoice with him in his wedding ceremony of baptism.

Why should the spiritual *result* be different where a person who has committed his life to Christ in faith is baptized within a very *short* time in response to that faith? In each situation, all the essential conditions are met. Can it possibly be that God penalizes false starts?

Are we to believe that salvation is dependent upon our having a "correct understanding" about how the process of salvation actually works? Does *any* of us have a perfectly "correct" understanding of how salvation actually works? Does any of us even have a full understanding of what makes a marriage?

Surely the process of salvation is too mystical and divine for any of us to presume to understand it perfectly.

Did those who were baptized on Pentecost have the same "theological understanding" as those who had the benefit of Paul's later letters in which the full implications of baptism were discussed?

In our choosing to be baptized, the important factor is the *purpose* for which we do it. And the purpose of every faith-motivated baptism is to *obey* Christ. Is it not the intent of every believer who is baptized to express his *submission* to the Lord Jesus Christ?

While there may be as many understandings of marriage as there are married couples, couples enter into marriage with the intent to make a permanent commitment to the relationship. They bring that commitment to the wedding ceremony. Likewise, understandings about the significance or dynamics of baptism may vary, even within fellowships accepting baptism as essential to the conversion process.

What matters most is not our *understanding* of the process, but our *purpose* in being baptized. When baptism is faith-motivated, as an act of obedience and as a loving response to what Christ has already done for us, then that purpose is clearly manifested. If we were wrong about the theological significance of the act, we were nevertheless right in submitting to it.

If we were not Christians at the moment we thought we were, we were nevertheless Christians when we proceeded to do all that Christ has asked us to do.

But a word of warning. Having suggested that delayed baptism for the right purpose may indeed complete our faith response to God, we must not continue to perpetuate theological distortion about the meaning, significance, and effect of baptism. How can we safely endorse a practice of delayed baptism that does not align with the New Testament pattern? How can we safely teach a belief that salvation is ours before submitting to an act that, according to Paul, puts us "into Christ."

Sorting Out Bad Timing

Salvation before baptism is bad timing theologically. But even in ordinary matters, we often have a way of sorting out bad timing. For example, even though a couple may have been living together before their wedding day, contrary to God's will, we nevertheless rejoice with them when they are finally married. It gives us all the more reason to rejoice! And the same is true when a birth out of wedlock is followed by the marriage of the parents. The stigma is mercifully lifted from the child who, after all, was innocent all along.

But finding a way to sort out bad timing does not close the book on the matter. If it is important to salvage bad timing, it is also important—and imperative—to *prevent* bad timing in the first place. And when we *can* do it, we *should* do it.

"Timing" in this case, of course, is really more a matter of sorting out grace from works. And the contest is not even close. Grace clearly wins out. But we must come to see that baptism (or even the mental act of faith, for that matter) is not a meritorious human "work," as if we could somehow *demand* that salvation be given to us because we have been dunked in a pool of water. Rather, baptism (like faith) is a matter of responding to God's grace in a manner that Christ has taught, commanded, personally demonstrated, and ordained.

As a loving response, baptism should be practiced exactly as it was practiced in the days of the apostles—*immediately,* as an integral part of the conversion experience, with all the joy and excitement of a wedding celebration.

Reflections

1. When it comes to the timing of biblical baptism, what pattern appears from the collage of examples given us in the New Testament?

2. How is that pattern different from the practice of many churches today?

3. Are there good reasons for delaying a believer's baptism? Would those same reasons have existed in the first century?

4. What does the practice of delayed baptism say about the significance of baptism?

5. How can baptism be safeguarded by "doing Bible things in Bible ways"?

6. Even if God should mercifully overlook "bad timing" relative to baptism, does it honor God to perpetuate a practice that departs from the biblical pattern?

7. Is delayed baptism merely "bad timing" or actually bad doctrine?

8. What message is conveyed when baptism follows immediately upon the heels of a faith commitment?

9. What are the pros and cons of waiting until a congregation has assembled for regular worship to perform a baptism?

10. Is waiting until there is a regular assembly consistent with the biblical pattern?

CHAPTER 7

WILL JUST ANY CEREMONY DO?

"But we, little fishes, after the example of our ICHTHYS (. . . Jesus Christ Son of God Savior) are born in water, nor have we safety in any other way than by permanently abiding in water."

Quintus Tertullian

Have you ever wondered how New Testament believers were baptized? What is baptism? Is it sprinkling, pouring, or full immersion? Does it make any difference?

The early Anabaptists, while insisting that adult baptism was essential, believed that pouring was sufficient. Some paintings in the early Christian era also depict baptism as a pouring. However, none of the earliest paintings goes back far enough in time to be conclusive.

Almost from the time infant baptism was initiated, sprinkling was the normal mode of this rite of initiation. The renowned theologian, Karl Barth, who himself rejected infant baptism, suggested that the Scriptures are indifferent on the question of the proper mode, but personally advocated immersion as more appropriately expressing what baptism is.

The wedding analogy does not make the method of baptism seem important. Does it matter, for example, whether a marriage is performed in a church building or in a private home? Does a wedding lose any significance if the ceremony occurs on a cruise ship, or under water, or several thousand feet above sea level in the gondola of a hot-air balloon? (There seems to be no end to the imagination of wedding couples!)

What's really important is not the venue but the sealing of the commitment, however it is done. And even if the traditional trappings of a wedding—the music, the flowers, the wedding gown and tuxedos, and perhaps even the rings—are missing, the formality of the simplest ceremony is sufficient to join the couple in holy matrimony.

Although it is tempting to conclude that the form of baptism is similarly of little consequence, several observations should be made before the issue is dismissed altogether.

Symbolism in a Burial

The first consideration is that, to the extent baptism is illustrative of Christ's death, burial, and resurrection, the most striking imagery would be seen in full immersion. When one is immersed, he or she is literally *buried* in the water, and literally *raised* in a kind of resurrection from that burial. In reflecting on the mode of sprinkling practiced in his day, Martin Luther was disturbed about both the visual and doctrinal implications:

> It is indeed correct to say that baptism is a washing away of sins, but the expression is too weak and mild to bring out the full significance of baptism which is rather a symbol of death and resurrection. For this reason I would have those who are to be baptized completely immersed in water as the Word says, and as the mystery indicates (*Luther's Works,* Vol. 36, p. 68).

Neither sprinkling nor pouring allows the full effect of the burial and resurrection symbolism. Yet that fact alone is not sufficient to force a conclusion about the proper mode. After all, the one who is being baptized will undoubtedly understand the act of baptism—however it is accomplished—to be a means of identifying with the risen Savior in His death, burial, and resurrection.

A passage from the letter to the Hebrews uses the word *sprinkling,* but not, surprisingly, regarding the outer washing of the body. Rather, it is applied to the inner cleansing of the heart, drawing an historic analogy to the sprinkling of the blood of animal sacrifices contrasted with Christ's own blood sacrifice:

> Therefore, brothers, since we have confidence to enter the Most Holy Place by the blood of Jesus, by a new and living way opened for us through the curtain, that is, his body, and since we have a great priest over the house of God, let us draw near to God with a sincere heart in full assurance of faith, *having our hearts sprinkled to cleanse us from a guilty conscience and having our bodies washed with pure water* (Hebrews 10:19-22).

The purity of the water is, of course, a reference to the purifying spiritual effect of baptism. It does not mean that the water itself is "holy water."

There are two important points. The first is the connection between an inward cleansing and an outward washing. The second is the contrast between "sprinkling" and "washing"—the latter being reserved for the outer symbolic cleansing. Or to put it another way, the only scriptural reference to "sprinkling" relates to the inner heart, not the act of water baptism.

In the many examples of New Testament converts, there is no indication of either sprinkling or pouring. When the scripture says that "both Philip and the eunuch went down into the water and Philip baptized him," it is possible that Philip could have dipped his hand down into the water in which they were standing and either sprinkled or poured a handful of water on the eunuch. (Movies about the life of Christ invariably show Jesus' own baptism like that.) But is that really probable? If sprinkling or pouring is all that Philip was going to do, why did they bother to get so wet? Why not just stand on the river bank and reach down for the water?

The Meaning of *Baptize*

Modern New Testament Greek scholars engage in an endless debate about the original meaning of the Greek word *baptizo*. It is a verb that, rather than being *translated* as sink, drown, go under, sink into, bathe, dip, or immerse—all of which would be accurate—has been *transliterated* (that is, simply put into a recognizable English form) in virtually every English translation.

Because sprinkling was an accepted mode of baptism at the time the King James Version was translated, this decision may have resulted from political concerns within the established church. Certainly it would have been embarrassing for the church had the word *baptizo* been translated consistently as "immerse." (A later, highly reputable but short-lived American translation that used the word *immersion* was referred to by some wags as the Immersion Version.)

Scholarly word studies can be the stuff of insufferable boredom. But wonderful little surprises can pop up from dusty lexicons. For example, the root word *bapto,* from which *baptizo is* derived, has as its primary meaning "to dip," and as its secondary meaning "to dye"—an obvious reference to what happens when something is dipped in a tinting substance. Although the secondary meaning of *bapto* is never itself used in connection with Christian baptism, from several scriptures we have learned that this combination of actions is precisely what happens in Christian baptism. This *symbolic* picture of "dipping" and "dying" corresponds perfectly with what we know about a *literal* act of immersion.

100

When we are dipped in the waters of baptism, we are penetrated through and through with the redeeming blood of Christ's sacrificial death. We take on the color of His righteous character so that, by His grace, we become like Him.

Naturally, this transformation does not exclusively or even primarily occur through the act of baptism. Our transformation takes place through a life of study, prayer, service, and sacrifice. But, because baptism associates us with the righteousness of Christ, who would want to be only partially "dyed" in Christ's likeness by anything less than a complete dipping?

Baptism of a different sort from water baptism can also lend some insight into the question of the word's meaning. For example, Peter defended his baptism of the Gentile centurion Cornelius by referring to the baptism of the Holy Spirit, both on the occasion of his meeting Cornelius and when the disciples themselves had been filled with the Spirit on Pentecost:

> As I began to speak, the Holy Spirit came on them as he had come on us at the beginning. Then I remembered what the Lord had said: "John baptized with water, *but you will be baptized with the Holy Spirit*" (Acts 11:15, 16).

Looking back to the descent of the Holy Spirit on the disciples at Pentecost, we see a graphic picture of baptism's meaning:

> When the day of Pentecost came, they were all together in one place. Suddenly a sound like the blowing of a violent wind came from heaven *and filled the whole house where they were sitting.* They saw what seemed to be tongues of fire that separated and came to rest on each of them. *All of them were filled with the Holy Spirit* and began to speak in other tongues as the Spirit enabled them (Acts 2: 1-4) .

No "sprinkling" of the Holy Spirit on this occasion! Quite to the contrary, there was a complete *engulfing,* an awesome display of God's divine power, which *overwhelmed* the disciples. And the word that describes this baptism of the Holy Spirit is the same as that which describes the wedding ceremony of water baptism. In the case of Cornelius, there is an almost simultaneous example of both kinds of baptism—first of the Holy Spirit, then of water.

What About Sprinkling or Pouring?

If either sprinkling or pouring were the original mode of baptism, several Scriptures would make little sense. A prime example is the mode of baptism used by John the Baptist. John baptized not only in the Jordan river (in which Jesus himself was baptized and then "went up out of the water"—Matthew 3:16), but also in other places where he could find a lot of water. We are told: "Now John also was baptizing at Aenon near Salim, *because there was plenty of water,* and people were constantly coming to be baptized" (John 3:23). If sprinkling or pouring were the form of his baptism, John could have gone about carrying a jug of water. As it is, John required large quantities of water for his baptisms.

On occasion, I find people wondering how 3,000 men and women were baptized on the day of Pentecost in Jerusalem. Was there really enough water to immerse that many people? Yes. Even today, there is evidence of more than enough water to baptize 3,000 people. In the maps in the back of your Bible, look at a schematic drawing of the city of Jerusalem in the first century. There are at least two enormous pools—the Pool of Siloam and the Pool of Bethesda. These pools, as well as others, facilitated the many ritual washings of the Jews during that time.

These washings were not simply polite sponge baths! The visitor to modern Israel can see Jews and Muslims completely dunking themselves in those ancient baptistries in the process of a number of ritual cleansings.

For example, one can still observe orthodox Jewish women ceremonially immersing at the end of their menstrual periods.

Given the thousands of people regularly cleansing themselves before entering into the temple, it is not difficult to see how the 3,000 could easily have been baptized in a single day.

No Confusion Among the First Converts!

These ritual washings also explain another curiosity to the modern mind: Why was there apparently no confusion about what the word *baptism* meant to those who lived in New Testament times? For example, when John the Baptist called for repentance and baptism, no one asked what that process was. Though it was not until later that John's disciples fully appreciated the difference between John's baptism and Jesus' baptism, neither baptism seems to have been the least bit ambiguous, novel, or odd to them.

When Jesus commanded His apostles to teach and baptize the nations, no apostle asked Jesus what He meant. And when Peter told the Pentecost crowd to repent and be baptized, it is unlikely that anyone questioned what Peter was calling them to do.

Those who heard the original words used in connection with baptism knew quite well what baptism was. It was what they all did periodically to purify themselves before God. The debate over the form of baptism distracts us from the obvious. First century converts took it to mean full immersion—a literal cleansing, a total washing.

A Spotty Historical Record

Linguistically, logically, and—most important—biblically, it is hard to define baptism as anything other than a complete dipping or a full immersion. Historically, widespread acceptance of something less than full immersion appeared only in the fifth or sixth century. While there were those who advocated sprinkling as early as the second century, especially for those unable to receive immersion, the idea encountered bitter resistance.

The first significant challenge to immersion came in the third century in the form of "clinical" baptism by pouring. While near death, a man by the name of Novatian asked for baptism in order to save his soul. Because he could not have survived the movement involved in full immersion, water was poured all around his body while he lay upon the bed.

From that time forward, there was snowballing acceptance of pouring or sprinkling, even when the baptism was unassociated with extraordinary circumstances. But how telling it is that so many centuries passed before sprinkling and pouring replaced the practice of immersion in the church.

In recent years, there has been renewed recognition of the significance of baptism by immersion in the Roman Catholic Church, arising from the work of the Second Vatican Council. Immersion is now encouraged as a fuller sign of baptism, as it pictures Christ's death, burial, and resurrection. Aidan Kavanagh, Catholic professor of liturgy at Yale University Divinity School, has commented favorably on this official reconsideration of baptism by immersion:

> Baptizing this way would be a welcome development—welcome because it might help restore something of the crucial and extraordinary nature of baptism to our consciousness, and some of the drastic robustness to baptismal symbolism, which for too long has been enfeebled by minimalism, privacy and the anonymity of the baptized (*Worship:* Vol. 48, No. 6).

The practical implementation of the Vatican's official encouragement toward baptism by immersion has seen little progress in the local parish church, owing—if for no other reason—to architectural incapacity. As more buildings of modern design are built with baptistries, rather than the traditional baptismal fonts, immersion may find its way into more common practice.

Why Settle for Less?

If water is involved at all, why not get the full treatment? Being painfully aware of just how spiritually dirty I am, I want to be absolutely spotless in the sight of the Lord. I am asking Jesus Christ to do nothing less than wash away my sins—all of them, every one, without exception. Like Naaman in the time of Elisha, I might not fully understand why God would ask me to go "dip in the river Jordan." The water itself has no cleansing power. But if the water baptism I read about in the New Testament symbolizes my spiritual regeneration, then I'll take all the water I can get.

An altogether different type of washing brings home the point. It happened when Jesus was teaching His apostles the need for humility by washing their feet:

> He came to Simon Peter, who said to him, "Lord, are you going to wash my feet?"
> Jesus replied, "You do not realize now what I am doing, but later you will understand."
> "No," said Peter, "you shall never wash my feet."
> Jesus answered, "Unless I wash you, you have no part with me."
> "Then, Lord," Simon Peter replied, *"not just my feet but my hands and my head as well!"* (John 13:6-9).

Even though, in the next verse, Jesus went on to explain that Peter was otherwise "clean," Peter had the right attitude in asking Jesus to wash his hands and his head as well. He wanted all the "washing" he could get if it meant that he would have a stronger relationship with Jesus. Likewise, if there is any link at all between the outer act of baptism and my inner cleansing, then wash me, Lord. Engulf me, Lord. Plunge me head to toe until I am pure in Your sight! Let the overflowing water of baptism flood my soul with Your saving grace!

Reflections

1. What is the proper method of baptizing if one is trying to associate it as closely as possible with its symbolism?

2. When Scripture (in both Old Testament and New) speaks of sprinkling, to what does it refer?

3. What was Martin Luther's view of the proper mode of baptism?

4. What is the meaning of the original Greek word for baptism?

5. Why do modern translations use the word "baptize"?

6. What can we learn from Holy Spirit baptism about water baptism?

7. Historically, when does it appear that pouring and sprinkling were first widely accepted as baptismal modes?

8. Why were pouring and sprinkling introduced?

9. What connection would there have been in the minds of first-century believers between the baptism of Jesus and both the ritual washings of the Jews and John's baptism?

10. If you have been immersed, what was the experience like, and how did you feel as you came up out of the water?

CHAPTER 8

THE UNION OF TWO SPIRITS

---

*"One of the great similarities between Christian-
ity and marriage is that, for Christians, they both
get better as we get older."*

Jean Rees

One of the popular wedding songs of the past few years reminds us that the ceremony is just the beginning of a relationship: "We've only just begun to live. White lace and promises. A kiss for luck and we're on our way. We've only just begun."

Thinking of baptism as the culmination of a faith experience would be as foolish as thinking that the wedding ceremony is the goal of a marriage. The real beauty of a marriage is not the flowers and candles at the wedding, but the slow, ever-growing, ever-deepening union of two souls. So it is with baptism. But how does that happen?

Another popular wedding song expresses the sentiment that goes to the heart of the marriage relationship: "The union of two spirits has caused us to remain, for wherever two or more of us are gathered in his name, there is love, there is love. . . . " That sentiment describes more than the wedding together of two spirits in a committed love relationship. It also describes the wedding ceremony of baptism in which the spirit of the believer is joined together with the Spirit of Christ.

Jesus talked about that union when He told Nicodemus about the new birth. "Unless a man is born of water and the Spirit, he cannot enter the kingdom of God." That's the familiar verse. But perhaps the more important verse follows. *"Flesh gives birth to flesh, but the Spirit gives birth to spirit"* (John 3:6).

Lest we focus too closely on the ceremony itself, it is important to remind ourselves that the essence of baptism is found in the committed love relationship with Christ. In marriage, of course, it is the relationship itself that brings the couple to the point of a wedding ceremony. And it is that same relationship that continues through the years to mature and to draw the couple closer and closer in spiritual unity.

That process of spiritual adhesion is true of baptism as well. It is one's faith relationship with Christ that brings the believer to the point of the wedding ceremony of baptism. But more important than this exciting beginning is the *spiritual growth* of the relationship we have with Christ.

Spiritual Rebirth Is the Key

In faith-responsive baptism, Jesus says we are born again— regenerated—in a mystical, yet very real, sense. It's as if we have a new spirit, the old one having been transformed. Through the threshold of baptism, we take on a new relationship that dramatically changes us. If love gives birth to a loving relationship in marriage, the Spirit of Christ gives birth to a new spirit within us in baptism. We are new people. We act and think differently. We have a new spiritual outlook.

Paul wrote to Titus about that newness:

> At one time we too were foolish, disobedient, de-
> ceived and enslaved by all kinds of passions and plea-
> sures. We lived in malice and envy, being hated and
> hating one another. But when the kindness and love of
> God our Savior appeared, he saved us, not because of
> righteous things we had done, but because of his
> mercy. He saved us through the washing of rebirth and
> renewal by the Holy Spirit, whom he poured out on us
> generously through Jesus Christ our Savior, so that,
> having been justified by his grace, we might become
> heirs having the hope of eternal life (Titus 3:3-8).

The water in a bath, shower, lake, or stream can bring
refreshment and cleansing of the outer body. But no matter how pure, clean, and exhilarating the water might
be, the inner person is not changed. In baptism, where
there is faith, repentance, and true commitment, the
water in the baptistry may even be dirty, but the inner
person is rapturously changed.

Not all couples "fall in love at first sight" and rush to
find a preacher. Similarly, not everyone who is baptized
experiences a dramatic change in life-style. Some will develop slowly even after baptism. Many others will have
been brought up to live exemplary lives. For one who has
grown up in a Christian home and formed an early relationship with God, baptism is not exactly sudden. It's
more like marrying the boy or girl next door whom you've
already fought with, befriended, and grown to love.

But all true believers should experience an immediate
dramatic change in their understanding of their own
spirituality. As someone has suggested, in baptism we do
not simply take on a new *capacity* for change toward
godliness; we are *actually changed!*

To be united with Christ in the likeness of His death,
for example, brings on the sobering realization that our
bodies are mortal, that our time on this earth is indeed
short, that what we would do in praise and service to the

Lord we must do now. To be raised from the waters of baptism in the likeness of Christ's resurrection brings the joyful reminder that our souls are prospectively immortal, that we will live beyond the grave, and that we will soon experience a life eternal where all of our present burdens will cease to exist.

The Holy Spirit Within Us

Naturally, this transformation of life and spiritual perspective cannot take place through our own efforts. As Jesus said, it is *Spirit* (God's Holy Spirit) that gives birth to our own spirituality. And as Paul told Titus, it is by the *Holy Spirit* that we are renewed.

The relationship between baptism and the work of the Holy Spirit is seen in John's prediction that the nature of his baptism would be surpassed by the nature of Christ's baptism. "I baptize you with water," said John, *"but he will baptize you with the Holy Spirit"* (Mark 1:8). John is obviously referring to something different and special about Jesus' baptism.

What could that different and special something be? It wouldn't be the form of Christ's baptism, because Jesus and John baptized in water in the same way. Nor would it be the forgiving significance of Christ's baptism, because both Jesus and John baptized for the forgiveness of sins. Apart from its forgiving *effectiveness,* that which is supremely special about Christ's baptism is the power of the Holy Spirit that it brings—a power that enriches the life of the Christian in a way that John's baptism could not.

The inaugural "baptism" of the Holy Spirit, of course, came on the day of Pentecost, and another special "baptism" of the Spirit came when Peter preached the gospel to Cornelius, the first Gentile convert. It may well be that John the Baptist's primary reference is limited to these special appearances of the Holy Spirit. But beyond these appearances is the more intimate manifestation of the Spirit for each of us. On a personal level, as Peter promised those who were baptized on the day of Pentecost, the Holy Spirit is given to Christians in a way that those baptized by John's baptism never experienced.

Although John's baptism of Jesus was a unique event, in it we see a prophetic picture of what would later take place in Christian baptism. Here baptism and the Holy Spirit are joined together, as seen in Mark's account:

> At that time Jesus came from Nazareth in Galilee and was baptized by John in the Jordan. *As Jesus was coming up out of the water, he saw heaven being torn open and the Spirit descending on him like a dove"* (Mark 1:9-11).

In his Gospel, the apostle John explains the significance of the appearance of the Holy Spirit at Jesus' baptism:

> Then John [the Baptist] gave this testimony: "I saw the Spirit come down from heaven as a dove and remain on him. I would not have known him, except that the one who sent me to baptize with water told me, *'The man on whom you see the Spirit come down and remain is he who will baptize with the Holy Spirit.'* I have seen and I testify that this is the Son of God" John 1:32-34).

We have already seen that through baptism we receive the gift of the Holy Spirit—not simply a specific "spiritual gift" or number of gifts, as such, but an actual indwelling of the Holy Spirit within us. What the Holy Spirit has specifically empowered individual Christians to do in His service is secondary to the *fact* of His presence. John's point is that, just as we have been engulfed in the waters of baptism, through Christ we are engulfed in the Holy Spirit.

Are Two Baptisms Required for the Spirit?

Just when we are jubilant about having the gift of the Holy Spirit, there are those who would pull us aside and tell us that our "one baptism" is not quite enough. Among

111

fellowships generally calling themselves "charismatic," many claim that it takes not one but *two* baptisms in order to receive the fullness of the Holy Spirit. The first baptism, usually in water, is frequently associated with the Holy Spirit, but only in a general sense, which rarely is well defined. The second baptism, of a spiritual nature, is often conferred by the laying on of hands and is for the purpose of receiving a special outpouring of the Holy Spirit.

While writing this book, I was often asked what project I was working on. When I said that I was writing a book on baptism, many people immediately responded, "You mean baptism of the Spirit?" They were surprised and curious that I was writing primarily about water baptism.

Their reaction confirms that many people do not associate the word *baptism* with the water baptism by which Jesus himself and New Testament Christians were baptized. That kind of baptism is all but forgotten in many Christian circles. What counts today is Holy Spirit baptism.

Among many believers today, any teaching of baptism is likely to be about an overwhelming of the Holy Spirit that one experiences wholly apart from water baptism. That "overwhelming" is a special feeling, happening on a memorable occasion, that manifests itself in the speaking in tongues or in some other dramatic demonstration of the Spirit's power.

For many, it is better felt than told. For others, it becomes the basis for heartfelt testimonies as to when they were saved or when they first became Spirit filled. But where do such experiences find their basis in Scripture? Are they biblical, or have we taken a wrong turn along the way?

A complete study of Holy Spirit baptism is another book. Suffice it to say that, according to current popular teaching, more than faith-responsive water baptism is needed before we fully receive the Holy Spirit. The teaching is based in large measure upon the circumstances found in Acts 8, where the Samaritans, although they had been baptized, had not received the Holy Spirit until Peter and John laid their hands upon them.

There, however, the added drama of the apostles' laying on of hands may well have been intended as a signal that the Samaritans—a hated people among the Jews—were just as acceptable in God's sight as were Jewish converts themselves. Or, indeed, the passage may simply reflect that no miraculous *signs* had come from the power of the Holy Spirit. After all, it was the power to perform those signs that Simon tried to buy from the apostles and for which he was soundly rebuked.

As we have already seen from numerous passages, reading into Acts chapter 8 the requirement of a two-step process for receiving the Holy Spirit would conflict with Acts chapter 2, where Peter announced the promise of God: "Repent and be baptized.... And you will receive the gift of the Holy Spirit"—no laying on of hands, no prayers, no *ifs, ands,* or *buts.* Whatever else they may have been, the events of Acts chapter 8 were clearly a special circumstances situation.

Second-Class Christians

Of even greater concern is the belief among many charismatic fellowships that anyone who is not "Spirit filled" (according to their definition) is not a complete Christian. Recently, while in England, I was asked to participate in an American radio talk show, via a transatlantic telephone hookup, regarding a book I had written on the New Age movement. Another guest was also being interviewed in the studio in the States. That guest later related to me an off-the-air comment made by the program's producer: "Dr. Smith writes excellent Christian books, but he's not Spirit filled."

To be "Spirit filled," according to some, is to have experienced a dramatic overwhelming of the Spirit, and to exercise some kind of supernatural spiritual gift—preferably speaking in tongues. While they are careful not to say so, the message clearly coming through is that there are two classes of Christians: First-Class Christians, who are "Spirit filled," and Second-Class Christians, who are not.

The Scriptures make no such classification of Christians. One is either a full-fledged Christian or he is not a Christian at all. There is simply no such thing as a Second-Class Christian. (Of course, a "full-fledged Christian" doesn't mean a "perfect Christian," because in truth we are all "erring Christians.")

As for being "Spirit filled," *every baptized believer* receives the Holy Spirit as the result of his turning to God. Nothing more is needed. Not a second baptism. Not an emotional experience. Not the laying on of anyone's hands. In short, there is no such thing as a Christian who is *not* "Spirit filled," unless, of course, one's life is lived in such a way as to snuff out the Spirit within him (Ephesians 5:15-18; 1 Thessalonians 5:19).

Being "Spirit filled" is having total intimacy with God. It is the spiritual consummation of the faith commitment we make to God. Believing that this spiritual consummation must await a second experience is like believing that the honeymoon must be delayed until the minister has laid his hands upon the marital bed. In New Testament baptism, all spiritual privileges attach to the conversion experience itself.

The exercise of spiritual gifts, especially the more dramatic ones, is not a test of one's relationship with the Holy Spirit. The judgment being made by many people is as superficial as one that says a husband and wife who don't hug and kiss each other in public like newlyweds aren't really in love! In truth, the emotional and the experiential are often pale substitutes for a deeper, quieter maturity.

Regrettably, in all of the clamor about being "Spirit filled," there is an arrogance unbefitting Christians. It is an arrogance Paul himself singled out for warning in his first letter to the Christians at Corinth, some of whom treated as second-class Christians those who did not have the same gifts as themselves. Paul goes to the heart of the problem when he writes: "There are different kinds of gifts, *but the same Spirit*" (1 Corinthians 12:4).

As for the notion that baptism alone is insufficient to make us "Spirit filled," Paul is strikingly instructive: "All these [special spiritual gifts] are the work of one and the same Spirit, and he gives them to each one, just as he determines" (1 Corinthians 12: 11) .

And how did we get that one Spirit? Was it by the laying on of hands? Was it by an experiential engulfing of the Holy Spirit sometime following our baptism? In writing about the divine, mystical role God plays when we respond to His grace through faith and baptism, Paul said: "The body is a unit, though it is made up of many parts; and though all its parts are many, they form one body. So it is with Christ. *For we were all baptized by one Spirit into one body . . . and we were all given the one Spirit to drink*" (1 Corinthians 12:12, 13).

Paul's point is that *spiritual gifts* are not to be equated with *receiving the Spirit*. All Christians receive the Spirit, but not all Christians speak in tongues. All Christians receive the Spirit, but not all Christians prophesy. All Christians receive the Spirit, but not all Christians have the gift of healing.

If what we all have in common is the Spirit, how did we all get it? Not all Christians, either in the first century or since, have had an ecstatic—"Pentecostal," if you will— spiritual experience. Nor have all Christians had holy hands laid upon them. The only common experience we have through which to receive the Spirit is water baptism.

Because we are all baptized into the same Spirit, no one has any right to boast of having received a greater blessing. Or of being more "Spirit filled" than another Christian. Or of being a Christian on a higher plane of acceptability before God. Such boasting has no place with the greatest of all gifts, love.

Since we are using the wedding ceremony as an analogy to baptism, it is ironic that Paul's warning regarding the Spirit and spiritual gifts should be the basis for one of the most frequently quoted passages in wedding ceremonies, the "love chapter" of 1 Corinthians 13.

May I suggest some relevant applications of Paul's message? "Love is patient [with those whose own spiritual lives have not yet fully matured], love is kind [when there are different views concerning spiritual gifts]. It does not envy [another's particular gifts in the Spirit], it does not boast [of whatever gift one has been given], it is not proud [so as to give the spiritually gifted cause for arrogance]. It is not rude [by forcing spiritual gifts as a test of spirituality], it is not self-seeking [in order to use whatever gift one has for his own purposes], it is not easily angered [by those who understand the Scriptures differently on the subject of Holy Spirit baptism], it keeps no record of wrongs [or score cards on who is winning the doctrinal arguments]" (1 Corinthians 13:4, 5).

When Peter promised the Holy Spirit to those who would repent and be baptized, he did not promise that all would speak in tongues. ("Are all teachers? Do all work miracles? Do all have gifts of healing? Do all speak in tongues?"—1 Corinthians 12:29, 30.) Nor did Peter add any *ifs* [if you have a thrilling emotional experience in the Lord], *ands* [and submit to the laying on of hands], or *buts* [but only for those who actually seek spiritual gifts]. Rather, as Paul wrote, "Where there are prophecies, they will cease; where there are tongues, they will be stilled" (1 Corinthians 13:8).

What Peter promised while speaking through the power of the Holy Spirit was that you and I can have the Spirit of God dwelling within us to aid in our growth toward spiritual maturity. What more could we ask of God? What more could we demand in others?

Spiritual! Not Just Religious

I agree with the charismatic fellowships when they say that being spiritual does not mean simply being religious. It is possible for one to be *religious* and never grasp what it means to be *spiritual*. For example, Paul told the philosophers on Mars Hill (Acts 17) that he perceived them to be "very religious." But they didn't have a clue about God, Jesus Christ, the Holy Spirit, our spiritual nature, or how God works in our lives through the power of the Spirit. In fact, the Greek word for "religious" here can also mean "superstitious."

True Christianity gets to the heart and substance of religion, which is spiritual service and spiritual living. It's not just a matter of paying lip service to one's relationship to Christ.

The husband who never fails to kiss his wife good-bye may, nevertheless, harbor a cold heart. Superficial commitment to a marriage will prevent marital maturity, and superficial commitment to Christ will prevent spiritual maturity. Baptism without spiritual growth would be the ultimate empty gesture.

On a more positive note, Paul reminds us of the fruit of the Spirit that will characterize our lives as we grow in our commitment to Christ:

> But the fruit of the Spirit is love, joy, peace, patience, kindness, goodness, faithfulness, gentleness and self-control. Against such things there is no law. Those who belong to Christ Jesus have crucified the sinful nature with its passions and desires. Since we live by the Spirit, let us keep in step with the Spirit (Galatians 5:22-25).

Is not this "fruit of the Spirit" also to be seen as *gifts* of the Spirit? As the bride of Christ, how richly we have been blessed!

It is said that couples who have lived together as husband and wife for many years tend even to start looking like each other. Whether this is actually true, it is true that in the process of spiritual growth, the maturing Christian will take on more and more of Christ's own characteristics. The wedding ceremony of baptism is truly just the beginning of our spiritual life in Christ.

A Wedding Miracle

The occasion of Jesus' first public miracle, a wedding celebration, illustrates the Christian's ever-growing spiritual relationship with Christ:

> On the third day a wedding took place at Cana in Galilee. Jesus' mother was there, and Jesus and his disciples had also been invited to the wedding. When the wine was gone, Jesus' mother said to him, "They have no more wine."
>
> "Dear woman, why do you involve me?" Jesus replied, "My time has not yet come."
>
> His mother said to the servants, *"Do whatever he tells you."*
>
> Nearby stood six stone water jars, the kind used by the Jews for ceremonial washing, each holding from twenty to thirty gallons.
>
> Jesus said to the servants, "Fill the jars with water"; so they filled them to the brim.
>
> Then he told them, "Now draw some out and take it to the master of the banquet."
>
> They did so, and the master of the banquet tasted the water that had been turned into wine. He did not realize where it had come from, though the servants who had drawn the water knew. Then he called the bridegroom aside and said, "Everyone brings out the choice wine first and then the cheaper wine after the guests have had too much to drink; but *you have saved the best till now"* John 2:1-10).

The analogy of baptism and a wedding ceremony is highlighted by the serendipity that Jesus began His ministry and performed His first miracle at a wedding celebration. Ministers correctly begin wedding ceremonies with a reference to the witnessing presence of God. In the example of Jesus, weddings receive His *personal* blessing.

So does the wedding ceremony of baptism. When we follow Mary's advice, "Do whatever he tells you," and in faith follow our Lord in the water of baptism, we are blessed with a miraculous transformation of our lives, like the changing of water to wine. No longer are we "without wine"—empty, lonely, unfilled. Our lives are not only filled to overflowing, but they are given the robustness of a changed life and a bouquet of inner peace and joy.

What about those who have experienced the wedding ceremony of baptism and the joys of being a Christian, but have also experienced the stress, strain, and struggle of the Christian walk? There are periods of disinterest and complacency in everyone's life. There are temptations to which we have succumbed—again and again. There are occasions of doubt and despair—perhaps even moments of anger at the God of our salvation. Christian leaders have failed us, Christian friends have disappointed us, and, worst of all, we have failed and disappointed ourselves.

Despite being a Christian, there are times when the wine is gone and we want to give up and walk off into a world which, even though it promises less, demands less. We tire of the struggle to be righteous and of the call to a level of spiritual thought and action that, at times, seems unattainable. As with the wedding feast at Cana, and with marriages themselves, the wine of our spirituality too often brings us to the bottom of the barrel.

What are we to do when our faith waivers, when our confession of Christ's lordship dissipates into a dissolute life, when the wedding ceremony of baptism seems but a remote act of idealistic commitment? Mary's words still call to us—"Do whatever he tells you."

> But seek first his kingdom and his righteousness, and all these things will be given to you as well (Matthew 6:33).

> Ask and it will be given to you; seek and you will find; knock and the door will be opened to you (Matthew 7:7).

> Love the Lord your God with all your heart and with all your soul and with all your mind and with all your strength . . . Love your neighbor as yourself (Mark 12:30, 31).

Simple teachings, really. Obvious things, one might think, like, "Husbands love your wives." But, when prayerfully and conscientiously applied, they bring about renewal and restoration.

He Saves the Best Till Last

God wants only the best for us, and He gives us the best at every point. But for those who remain steadfast and faithful to Christ over a lifetime of love and service, the story of the wedding feast contains a picture of a special blessing. As with the wine, He saves the very best till last.

Surely few couples have the foggiest notion of the tests to which their wedding vows will be put during the course of their marriage. Even the most serious and introspective fail to anticipate the worst they might have to experience. The loss of a home, acts of unfaithfulness, perhaps even the death of a child. Yet for those whose commitment is certain and whose resolve is firm, the end is much better than the beginning.

And that's to be expected even more so in one's relationship with Christ. The wedding ceremony of baptism is only a beginning. Through the power of the Holy Spirit working with grace in our lives, the end is better than the beginning.

And that should be no mystery. Christ saves the best till last!

Reflections

1. What inner transformation is supposed to occur when a believer is baptized in water?

2. What was promised to those on Pentecost as a result of their faith-responsive baptism?

3. What is the difference between *gifts* of the Holy Spirit and *the gift* of the Holy Spirit?

4. What two baptisms did Cornelius experience? In what order of time?

5. Does every believer experience those same two baptisms?

6. How were spiritual gifts, such as tongues and prophecy, generally received in the days of the apostles?

7. What should be our attitude toward differences regarding spiritual gifts?

8. Apart from the more Pentecostal-type gifts like tongues and prophecy, are there spiritual gifts for every believer?

9. In what way is the act of baptism like Jesus' miracle of turning water to wine?

10. In what ways has your relationship with God since your baptism demonstrated that "He saves the best until last"?

CHAPTER 9

INFANT BAPTISM—A SHOTGUN WEDDING?

"Baptism seemed such an integral part of New Testament Christianity and I couldn't imagine a droplet of water dribbled on my head when I was a baby could be a proper substitute for that adult symbol of submission and obedience."

Cliff Richard

To this point, our discussion of baptism has assumed sufficient maturity for a person to choose his or her participation in the act. But if you were baptized as an infant, your experience will have been distinctly different. Both today and in centuries past, the most widely-held view of baptism among the Christian community sees baptism as being unquestionably essential, but it raises the thorniest of all the problems associated with baptism. By this view, it is proper to administer the rite of baptism to infants shortly after their birth. Fellowships following this view of baptism do not exclude adult baptism for those considered to be converts, but typically baptize most of their adherents as infants.

When Did Infant Baptism Begin?

The history of infant baptism dates back to at least the latter part of the second century. It was known at the time of Origen and Tertullian, though Tertullian opposed it on the grounds that it would be safer and more profitable to wait until faith was formed in the believing adult. Because Origen wrote that "the Church has received a tradition from the Apostles to give baptism even to little children," it has been assumed by many that the practice is in fact biblical.

Augustine's approval of the practice in the fourth century led the way to wholesale acceptance of the practice. Augustine (A.D. 353-430) believed that infant baptism canceled the guilt of original sin, but did not eliminate man's sinful nature. He taught that unbaptized children were spiritually lost.

Because a child could not possess the penitent faith of New Testament converts, the Roman Catholic Church finally dismissed altogether any need for subjective, personal faith by infants, choosing instead to regard baptism as a holy sacrament, effective simply because it is done.

This position, best described as *baptismal regeneration,* served both to cancel assumed original sin and to initiate the infant into the church. Thus justified, infant baptism came to be a virtually unquestioned practice of the Roman Church by the middle of the seventh century.

During the Reformation, the Catholic view of baptism continued with only minor variations on the theme. Luther felt infant baptism was proper, but had great difficulty finding a biblical rationale to accommodate the infant's obvious lack of prerequisite faith. At the end of his life, he still professed ignorance on the issue. Calvin saw infant baptism as the Christian equivalent of circumcision for infants born of believing parents. He said such infants were "children of the covenant."

Calvinists have been divided on the troublesome issue of how infants can be said to have faith. Some believe that faith is instilled in the child by the Holy Spirit at the moment of the child's baptism, while others believe that baptism raises a presumption of regeneration that might later be rebutted by the rejection of Christianity on reaching adulthood.

From the time infant baptism became an established practice in the fourth century until the period of the Reformation, the practice was largely unchallenged. The only controversy was how it all worked out in religious theory. The first major departure from the practice came in the sixteenth century when the Anabaptists rejected the practice of infant baptism because they believed that an infant could not have faith.

Since then, there have been small skirmishes among the Christian community, but infant baptism has more than held its own and is today the most widely-practiced view of baptism. At the risk of replowing ground that has been tilled for centuries, there is no way to avoid the issue if we are fully to understand the subject of baptism.

The Notion of Original Sin

As suggested in the foregoing brief history of infant baptism, the practice has two basic doctrinal justifications: first, the idea of baptismal regeneration to cancel original sin; and second, the concept that infants who are "children of the covenant" are entitled to be baptized. In this chapter, we will discuss the idea of original sin, but it must be recognized that not all who practice infant baptism justify it on the basis of original sin. Nor do all who believe in original sin practice infant baptism.

There are various understandings of original sin, but they typically assume that infants inherit sin and its curse through their parents and their parents' parents, all the way back to Adam and Eve. Use of the word *sin*, as opposed to its plural, *sins*, is significant. It is not al-

125

ways clear whether what is inherited is a *sinful nature* characteristic of all mankind or the actual, specific (count them, name them) *sins* of the child's parents, grandparents, great grandparents, and so on.

Practically, original sin means that a child is spiritually vulnerable in the event of an early death. Whether an unbaptized infant who died would actually end up in hell, however, has been a matter of debate.

It is important to stress that not all who believe in original sin believe in infant damnation. In fact, fewer and fewer do. The Roman Catholic Church, for example, has all but rejected the idea of limbo, which at one time was thought to be the assigned destiny of unbaptized infants. Limbo, which was never officially adopted as Church doctrine, was a contrived compromise between heaven and hell, a shadowy in-between state of existence invented to avoid the stinging possibility of eternal punishment for unbaptized babies.

Today, some priests will admit that, even though the Church has largely abandoned the notion of infant damnation, the average parishioner hasn't got the message. Mothers and fathers still bring their babies to be baptized out of fear of the spiritual consequences for unbaptized babies. The Church has practiced infant baptism for this reason for so long that recent attempts at a reversal in practice have encountered stubborn resistance.

Unfortunately, while infant damnation is becoming less and less popular, the notion of original sin itself lives on among both Catholics and Protestants. For that reason, the remainder of this chapter is devoted to an in-depth review of this widely held doctrine.

Because original sin is such a pervasive belief among the Christian community, it is impossible to skip lightly over it. However, I recognize that a detailed discussion of the doctrine of original sin will not be everyone's cup of tea. If that includes you, you may prefer to proceed at this point to the next chapter. Even if you are not particularly drawn to the doctrine of original sin, should you choose to stay with us, I believe you will find the discussion to be more interesting than the topic might initially suggest. After all, there must be *some* reason why so many people believe that we are born spiritually tainted.

Did the Apostle Paul Teach Original Sin?

The principal New Testament Scripture from which the doctrine of original sin is derived is found in Paul's letter to the Romans, in chapter 5. There, Paul contrasts the sin of Adam (which brought death) with the salvation of Christ (which brings life). The implication, supposedly, is that you and I are burdened with sin and death because of Adam.

While reading the passage, it is helpful to ask whether Paul is referring to *sin itself* or to the *consequence* of sin—namely death—as that which we receive. And, if death, is Paul referring to *physical* death or *spiritual* death?

> Therefore . . . sin entered the world through one man, and death through sin, and in this way death came to all men, because all sinned....
>
> Consequently, just as the result of one trespass was condemnation for all men, so also the result of one act of righteousness was justification that brings life for all men. For just as through the disobedience of the one man the many were made sinners, so also through the obedience of the one man the many will be made righteous.
>
> The law was added so that the trespass might increase. But where sin increased, grace increased all the more, so that, just as sin reigned in death, so also grace might reign through righteousness to bring eternal life through Jesus Christ our Lord (Romans 5:12, 18-21).

After reading this passage, we can appreciate what Peter said about Paul: "His letters contain some things that are hard to understand . . ." (2 Peter 3:16).

Paul's first letter to the Corinthians contains a brief, clear summary of what Paul wrote to the Romans. "For since death came through a man, the resurrection of the dead comes also through a man. For as in Adam all die, so in Christ all will be made alive" (1 Corinthians 15:21, 22).

This passage indicates that what is inherited from Adam is the *consequence* of sin—namely, death. That fits in the context of the Corinthian letter, which addresses the nature of death and the resurrection. In addition to the physical *consequence* of sin, Paul turns in his Roman letter to the matter of *sin itself* and how we are justified by Christ's righteousness.

For Paul, the resolution of the issue came later in the same Roman letter. In discussing a somewhat different issue (regarding obsolescence of the law of circumcision and the law of Moses), Paul coincidentally infers that there is in fact an important prerequisite to any sin: an awareness of God's law— whether it be the law of Moses or the law of grace in Christ.

> Indeed *I would not have known what sin was except through the law.* For I would not have known what coveting really was if the law had not said, "Do not covet." But sin, seizing the opportunity afforded by the commandment, produced in me every kind of covetous desire. For apart from law, sin is dead. *Once I was alive apart from law;* but when the commandment came, sin sprang to life and I died (Romans 7:7-9).

Paul's understanding of his own spiritual condition is the best commentary on the difficult passage he had written just two chapters earlier. Before he was aware of God's laws, says Paul in a spiritual double-entendre, he was spiritually *alive* (without sin) and free from the condemnation of spiritual death that comes through disobedience to God. There was no sin in Paul's life until he *knew* the law and then chose to disobey it. Paul rejects the idea that we are burdened with sin prior to familiarity with God's commandments.

This does not mean, of course, that those who are unaware of the law of Moses or of Christian doctrine are blissfully ignorant and free from the need for salvation. Paul isn't putting missionaries out of a job. In his Roman letter, Paul addresses this very concern: "All who sin apart from the law will also perish apart from the law. . ." (Romans 2:12). The apostle continues,

> Indeed, when Gentiles, who do not have the law, do by nature things required by the law, they are a law for themselves, even though they do not have the law, since they show that the requirements of the law are written on their hearts, their consciences also bearing witness, and their thoughts now accusing, now even defending them (Romans 2:14, 15).

To Paul, "knowing the law" refers, at a minimal level, to a universal awareness of right and wrong in the spiritual realm. There is a level on which everyone, regardless of the particular religion of his or her culture, is morally aware and in need of salvation. But this level assumes a degree of moral maturity beyond infancy.

Sin does not operate in a vacuum. Sin is failure or refusal to do what we know to be right in God's sight. If we do not have the maturity to know basic morality, we are incapable of sin. If we are incapable of sin, we are not accountable for sin.

What, If Anything, Do We Inherit?

What have we inherited from Adam? His *personal* sins? Surely not. Perhaps the word *inherit* is misleading. Paul never uses that word in his discussion. He simply suggests that Adam was the first man to sin and the first to incur the sentence of physical death. He does not suggest that we are born with sin attached to our umbilical cord.

Paul affirmed that there is a way in which we follow in Adam's footsteps. Like Adam, we are sinful creatures. Our sinful nature follows from our Creator-given freedom of choice between good and evil. God did not create us to be sinful, but, in bestowing upon us the freedom to choose, He has created the risk that we may choose wrongly. If we have something in common with Adam, it's our *capacity* for sin—yes, even our *tendency* to sin— our carnal self.

If by "original sin" we mean our *sinful nature,* then original sin is biblical. But the passages that discuss our sinful nature (e.g., Job 4:17; 14:4; Ephesians 2:3) all assume moral maturity beyond infancy. A two-month-old child who inherits a million dollars is not given immediate control over it. That will have to wait until he is old enough to manage it responsibly. While the infant might be called a millionaire, he would not be held accountable for what happens to his money at so young an age.

Likewise, we are not held accountable for our sinful nature until we have matured sufficiently to be aware of the choices to be made in a spiritual realm. We must carefully distinguish between having a *sinful nature,* for which ultimately we need salvation, and inheriting *sin,* for which some say we need to be baptized as infants. The former is true; the latter is false.

A very human apostle Paul, in marked contrast to his highly theoretical discussion regarding Adam and Christ, spoke with candor and moral agony about his struggle with sin:

> I do not understand what I do. For what I want to do I do not do, but what I hate I do. And if I do what I do not want to do, I agree that the law is good. As it is, it is no longer I myself who do it, but *it is sin living in me.* I know that nothing good lives in me, that is, *in my sinful nature* (Romans 7:15-18).

Everyone has experienced what Paul is talking about. On any day of the week, I could echo Paul's cry of anguish, "What a wretched man I am!" (Romans 7:24).

King David, after his sin with Bathsheba and the murder of her husband, experienced that abject feeling of moral self-embarrassment. This very feeling led David to employ poetic hyperbole, saying that he was sinful from the very point of his conception!

> Have mercy on me, O God,
>   according to your unfailing love;
> according to your great compassion
>   *blot out my transgressions.*
> Wash away all my iniquity
>   and cleanse me from my sin.
>
> *For I know my transgressions,*
>   and my sin is always before me.
> Against you, you only, have I sinned
>   and done what is evil in your sight,
> so that you are proved right when you speak
>   and justified when you judge.
> *Surely I was sinful at birth,*
>   *sinful from the time my mother conceived me*
>   (Psalm 51:1-5).

Other translations confuse the meaning of the passage. The King James Version, for example, renders verse 5 as: "Behold, I was shapen in iniquity; and in sin did my mother conceive me."

However one interprets either translation, David's point is not that he could specifically identify any particular sins of his father, his mother, or even himself while in his mother's womb. Nor was he condemned by a more generic "sinful nature" such that, had he been stillborn, his soul would have been in spiritual jeopardy. Rather, he is so painfully conscious of his sin that he feels it ingrained in his very being.

Referring to his "transgressions," David recognizes that, as John said, "sin is lawlessness" (1 John 3:4). While in his mother's womb, or even as a child, David would not have known the law. Not until he knew the law and transgressed its commands did David actually commit sin. But knowing that to be true in some acade-

131

mic sense didn't stop him from *feeling* as if he had violated it from the moment of his conception.

In another psalm, David talks about the seemingly natural inclination of the wicked from the time they are born: "Even from birth the wicked go astray; *from the womb they are wayward and speak lies*" (Psalm 58:3). David is not referring to any sin a person might passively *inherit* from those who have gone before him or to a more generalized "sinful nature" that condemns a person from the moment of birth—simply the character that happens to be formed as the result of one's own active sins.

Here, too, David indulges in poetic license when he refers to infants *speaking* lies "from the womb." Newborn infants obviously do not speak, whether lies or truth. As the context indicates, David is intimating with righteous anger that the despicable rulers have been wicked all their lives.

Are Specific Sins Passed Down?

Some have suggested that children who exhibit a particular evil bent do so as the direct result of that same character flaw in the parents and, predictably, in more distant predecessors. As an example of *specific sins* passed from one generation to another, they cite the sin of dishonesty, as first seen in Abraham and later in his son Isaac, his grandson Jacob, and finally in the great grandsons who lied to Jacob about Joseph.

This mimicking of specific sins is offered as proof of the penalty attached to violations of the law of Moses:

> . . . for I, the Lord your God, am a jealous God, punishing the children for the sin of the fathers to the third and fourth generation of those who hate me, but showing love to a thousand generations of those who love me and keep my commandments (Exodus 20:5, 6).

Are we to believe that Abraham, the great patriarch of faith and spiritual father of us all, is included in the category of "those who hate me?" This seems unlikely. And consider David. Despite his own great sin, David was hardly a God-hater!

While a literal application of the first part of the passage might prove inherited evil tendencies, an equally literal reading of the second part would suggest that, where there are two righteous parents, their offspring for a thousand generations would also be righteous. No one contends that has ever happened!

A virtually identical passage about the blessings and curses under the law of Moses focuses on the word *punishment*:

> The Lord, the Lord, the compassionate and gracious God, slow to anger, abounding in love and faithfulness, maintaining love to thousands, and forgiving wickedness, rebellion and sin. Yet he does not leave the guilty unpunished; *he punishes the children and their children for the sin of the fathers to the third and fourth generation* (Exodus 34:6, 7).

The idea of "punishment" (better understood as having to endure the consequences) is separated from the actual "sin of the fathers." Punishment does not mean that, through some combination of biological and spiritual laws, the children receive in themselves their fathers' specific sins. Rather, the fathers, through their sins, tend to bring adverse *consequences* upon their offspring.

We can see how it happened, for example, to the sons and daughters in Israel and Judah at the time of the divided kingdom. Because of the parents' sin of idolatry, even the young were killed or captured by the Assyrians and Babylonians. Many were led away to exile in a foreign land. Had they done anything to merit that consequence of sin?

The child of a violent or drunk parent all too often suffers abuse at the hands of that parent without any fault on the child's part. And the child of a mother who is a drug addict may come into this world experiencing withdrawal symptoms.

Sins do have consequences in the lives of innocent parties. But it is another thing altogether to say that the *sin,* as opposed to the *consequence,* is somehow passed on.

If specific sins are *not* inherited, then how are we to explain generation after generation of perpetuated sin, such as the dishonesty seen in Abraham's family? Is that merely coincidence? Probably not.

Personality traits, which are almost as identifiable as physical traits, do pass from one generation to the next. For example, I not only look much like my father, and walk and talk as he walked and talked, but I also share his personality and emotional temperament. But shared personality traits, as such, do not bring sin into our lives. My sisters and I have the same parents, yet we do not always share our parents' spiritual struggles, nor each other's.

A well-known proverb explains why a person might possess the same spiritual weaknesses as his parents: "Train a child in the way he should go, and when he is old he will not turn from it" (Proverbs 22:6). Unfortunately, that proverb is as true in the negative sense as it is in the positive. Because parental training is as much a matter of example as anything else, it is no accident that children tend to mimic their parents morally as well as otherwise.

The child from a home where there's lots of swearing going on is likely to develop a foul mouth at an early age, and many abused children grow up to abuse their own children in the same way. This is the sense in which we often say, whether positively or negatively, "Like father, like son."

We must not confuse either *personality traits* (which may be influenced by genetic reproduction) or *character traits* (which may be acquired from parental teaching and example) with *specific* sins, which each person commits individually and personally.

Ezekiel Disclaimed the Idea of "Inherited Sin"

Acknowledging that we have a sinful nature common to all humankind does not admit that we actually inherit sin for which we are held accountable at the moment of our birth, and for which one should immediately be baptized.

In a strongly-worded, profound discussion of the issue of sin by inheritance, the prophet Ezekiel says repeatedly that each person is held accountable only for his own sins:

> What do you people mean by quoting this proverb about the land of Israel:
>
> "The fathers eat sour grapes, and the children's teeth are set on edge"?
>
> As surely as I live, declares the Sovereign Lord, you will no longer quote this proverb in Israel. For every living soul belongs to me, the father as well as the son—both alike belong to me. *The soul who sins is the one who will die* (Ezekiel 18:1-4). (See also Jeremiah 31:29, 30).

Ezekiel goes on to list eight *specific sins* that a particular father does *not* commit. Then he lists the same eight specific sins that *are* committed by his son. Finally, Ezekiel once again lists the same eight sins that are *not* committed by the son's son. According to Ezekiel, sin is not received involuntarily from one's parents, or from Adam, like some hereditary disease.

> Yet you ask, "Why does the son not share the guilt of his father?" Since the son has done what is just and right and has been careful to keep all my decrees, he will surely live. *The soul who sins is the one who will die. The son will not share the guilt of the father, nor will the father share the guilt of the son.* The righteousness of the righteous man will be credited to him, and the wickedness of the wicked will be charged against him (Ezekiel 18:19, 20).

It is disappointing how many authors writing in support of the idea of original sin ignore Ezekiel's clear teaching, and don't even attempt to reconcile it with their view. This passage alone ought to answer the question of whether the newborn infant inherits the sins of his predecessors.

Nor was Ezekiel's teaching either revolutionary or exceptional. The ancient principle was stated clearly and concisely in the law of Moses: "Fathers shall not be put to death for their children, nor children put to death for their fathers; *each is to die for his own sin*" (Deuteronomy 24:16).

Despite the inevitability of future sin, the infant is born with a clean slate. Should the infant die, no adverse spiritual consequences whatever would befall that precious soul.

What Did Jesus Say About Original Sin?

There were those in Jesus' day, even among His disciples, who believed in some form of original sin. Remember the question Jesus was asked about the man who was blind from birth? "Rabbi, who sinned, this man or his parents, that he was born blind?" (John 9:2).

They believed that the man's blindness was the result of sin that existed prior to his birth—sin which he inherited from his parents or sin he himself had committed either in a preexistent state or while yet in the womb!

But Jesus refutes both of those notions about the existence of sin at birth. "'Neither this man nor his parents sinned,' said Jesus 'but this happened so that the work of God might be displayed in his life'" (John 9:3). Obviously, Jesus did not say that the man's parents were sinless. Rather, He said that any sins they had committed were not transmitted to their son with physical consequences.

Later in the same incident, the Pharisees demonstrated their belief in original sin when they angrily responded to the then-healed man who was defending Jesus: "To this they replied, 'You were steeped in sin at birth; how dare you lecture us!'" (John 9:34). When Jesus suggested that spiritual, not physical, blindness is the real problem in the world, the Pharisees asked, "What? Are we blind too?" (John 9:40).

Jesus' response flatly denied any notion of original sin. In effect, what Jesus said was this: blindness doesn't come from sin; rather, sin comes from blindness. Jesus was plainly telling them that no physical impairment, whether blindness or anything else, is the result of inherited sin. And the same is true of moral impairment. Moral guilt comes only when one is mature enough to "see" what is right morally, and then chooses to close his eyes to it. The blind man had *not* been steeped in sin at birth, as they had supposed. Nor is anyone.

Original Sin or Sinful Nature?

Having seen that *specific sins* are not inherited, we should address the issue of whether there is a *sinful nature* that is inherited. As humans, we inherit *all* our human traits, including the ability to choose. And the ability to choose between good and evil is at the heart of sin, for sin is choosing to do evil. So if by the term *original sin* we mean the ability to choose wrongfully, then we are close to the truth. But only close.

Merely having the *ability* to choose evil does not mean that one *has* chosen evil. Certainly, a newborn infant has had no opportunity to make any decisions, whether good or evil. Therefore, saying that *at the moment of birth* one has "inherited" a sinful nature that requires immediate baptism draws a faulty conclusion. Simply because one has the ability to choose does not mean that he is spiritually defiled by choices he never made.

The best example of that principle is Jesus Christ, of whom Isaiah prophesied: "He will eat curds and honey *when he knows enough to reject the wrong and choose the right*" (Isaiah 7:15). Like all other infants, Jesus was blameless until He was mature enough to choose right

137

from wrong. Of course, even when Jesus matured to the point that He could make evil choices, He never yielded to the temptation. Hence, though He "has been tempted in every way, just as we are—yet [He] was without sin" (Hebrews 4:15). Naturally, Jesus was unique in never choosing evil. But, as a sinless child, He was not unique. Moral accountability does not attach to any child until he *"knows enough to reject the wrong and choose the right."*

Was Jesus Born With Original Sin?

Whatever the definition of original sin—whether inherited *specific* sins or a *generic* "sinful nature" that attaches spiritual guilt at the moment of birth—our reference to Jesus raises a troubling question: If there really is original sin, how could Jesus Christ himself have been sinless? Traditionally, the Christian community has acknowledged that Jesus was fully human but that He, and He alone, was safeguarded from a sinful nature because He was conceived by the Holy Spirit without the contribution of a human father.

The force of the question has driven some to contrive the "doctrine of concupiscence," a twenty-five-cent theological term meaning that sin is passed on through the lust of sexual relations. Because Jesus was conceived by the Holy Spirit, it is argued that no sin passed to Jesus.

It's a convenient argument, but nowhere in Scripture is there a hint that sin is transmitted through the lust of sexual relations, as if it were a spiritual version of AIDS. Jesus was not sinless simply because He was conceived miraculously. He was sinless because—like you and me—He was born without sin and—unlike you and me— thereafter *did* no sin.

How Jesus could exist as both God and man is a mystery. Those of us who believe that Jesus is God incarnate accept Jesus' humanity as much as His divinity, for He is referred to in Scripture, not only as the "Son of God," but frequently as the "Son of Man."

Though conceived in Mary by the power of the Holy Spirit, Jesus was, nevertheless, the son of Mary in the flesh. Like the rest of us, Jesus was a descendant of Adam. Luke was careful to point out that fact in his genealogy of Jesus, which, despite a reference to Jesus' legal father Joseph, actually traces Jesus' ancestry through Mary, His natural mother.

> He was the son, so it was thought, of Joseph,
> the son of Heli, the son of Matthat . . .
> the son of David, the son of Jesse . . .
> the son of Isaac, the son of Abraham . . .
> the son of Noah, the son of Lamech . . .
> the son of Seth, *the son of Adam* . . . (Luke 3:23-38).

Though Joseph did not contribute to Jesus' birth, Mary did! And her lineage is traced to the same Adam through whom "sin entered the world." If Cain and Abel and Seth were born with the guilt of Adam's sin, and so were their children and their far-distant descendants, including Mary, then Jesus would also have been born with the same condemned "sinful nature." Exempting Jesus from a sinful birth pays only lip service to His humanity and denies the reality of it. It is convenient to say that Jesus, being the Son of God, was an exception to humanity's "sinful nature," but it robs Him of His complete identity with humankind. It says He was God in the flesh, but not *really!*

The truth is that Jesus was not an exception at all. Like every other person ever born, Jesus was born with a human nature—that is, with the *capacity* for sin. But He did not come from the womb *condemned* by sin, nor did we.

An Immaculate Conception?

Roman Catholics believe that there was a dramatic break in the human chain from Adam to Jesus, and that Mary is the key to how Jesus could have been born without original sin. Perplexed over how to have a sinless

Son of God without contradicting the notion of original sin, the Roman Catholic Church rationalized that Mary herself must have been born without sin—hence the lack of original sin in her son Jesus.

Using a veiled reference to the offspring of a woman who would do battle with Satan (Genesis 3:15), the Church maintained that Mary was given a special blessing as the "Mother of God"—a term first used in A.D. 320—to be sinless, both in her own conception and throughout her life. Therefore, her son was able to escape the original sin with which the rest of us are born.

Nowhere, of course, does Scripture mention Mary's so-called immaculate conception, or hint that she lived a sinless life. Not until at least the third century did this speculative idea surface among Catholics. And despite widespread acceptance of the belief for many centuries, it was only as recently as 1854 that Pope Pius IX declared this belief to be official dogma.

This unbiblical dogma is correct about Mary's immaculate conception, if you discard the claim that it's a special blessing reserved only for Mary and Jesus. Mary's conception *was* immaculate. So was Jesus' conception. And so was yours! *All of us* were born of an immaculate conception. *All of us* were born absolutely pure and sinless. Mary and Jesus were not exceptions, but the rule to which there are no exceptions.

Rather than invent an unscriptural fable about Mary, who was indeed blessed among women and worthy of great honor, we should examine the false doctrine of original sin that made that fable necessary.

Protestants rightly reject the "immaculate conception" of Mary. Yet, because many still hold the doctrine of original sin, the problem remains of a sinless Savior born with sin. Applying the notion of original sin to Jesus Christ gives entirely new meaning to the sentiments expressed in "Away in the Manger" or "Silent Night." Little baby Jesus—born with original sin?

An Appeal to Our Moral Senses

One of the things that makes a newborn baby so special to us is its very innocence, its purity. Those wrinkly, little one-day-old faces don't mask sinful souls! If they did, surely Jesus would not have told Nicodemus that we must be "born again." *Born* again, only to be *filled* again with sin from the point of that new beginning?

If a newborn baby is burdened with sin as he comes into the world, is it likely that Jesus would have chosen the metaphor of being "born again" to explain to Nicodemus his need to be redeemed? If original sin were a spiritual truth, would not some other metaphor have been more accurate?

Reflect for a moment on the nature of the loving God of heaven. How does what we know of Him support the proposition that if a baby were to die without baptism, he or she would be in spiritual jeopardy? Could the God you know from the Scriptures and from your own Christian experience condemn to Hell an unbaptized infant? Is it remotely possible that God's condemning judgment would extend to children who don't even realize there is a God, or that He has given spiritual and moral laws to obey?

We are embarking on dangerous waters to subjectively speculate about God's judgment. For example, asking whether a loving God could condemn to hell a morally compelling nonChristian (some would suggest Mahatma Gandhi) is an equally difficult question, but it is a different question. The child, by comparison, cannot make any choices about what he believes or who he will be religiously. It is altogether morally unthinkable that God's character could allow Him to condemn to hell souls who, by reason of incapacity, could never understand the gospel even if they were exposed to it!

But Didn't Jesus Bless the Little Children?

Support for infant baptism is claimed from the occasion of Jesus' blessing the little children. The point is made that, because Jesus did not exclude children from His kingdom, He therefore cast His blessing on infant baptism. Actually, the passage tells us the exact opposite from that. The children were not brought to Jesus in order for Jesus to baptize them, despite the fact that Jesus' disciples *were* baptizing adults who believed on Him. Why, then, were they brought? "Then little children were brought to Jesus *for him to place his hands on them and pray for them.* But the disciples rebuked those who brought them" (Matthew 19:13).

Jesus was *praying* for the children—not baptizing them. Rather than supporting infant baptism, this incident prompts several compelling lessons about the *innocence* of children:

> When Jesus saw this, he was indignant. He said to them, "Let the little children come to me, and do not hinder them, for the kingdom of God belongs to such as these. I tell you the truth, anyone who will not receive the kingdom of God like a little child will never enter it." And he took the children in his arms, put his hands on them and blessed them (Mark 10:14-16).

Jesus' primary lesson may have been to show that the kingdom of Heaven is for those who trust Jesus in the same totally dependent way that a little child trusts. It is a comparison between children's position of powerlessness and utter dependence upon their parents and the would-be believer's need to recognize his own helplessness when it comes to salvation and his utter dependence upon his Heavenly Father.

Jesus' secondary lesson may have been that God loves even the "insignificant" of this world. Until they reached maturity, children in that culture were considered only property, particularly by their fathers.

Beyond those two lessons, if Jesus is telling us anything about the spiritual condition of children, is it that they are full of sin and condemned? To the contrary, by implication, He is telling us that they are *without* sin, for if children are full of sin, then Jesus' teaching about the kingdom makes no sense at all. The kingdom of God belongs to those who are like children. Does it make sense that the kingdom of God belongs to unregenerate sinners?

Far from teaching that children need to be baptized like adults, Jesus' teaching here implies that adults need to be spiritually regenerated as if they were children. Born again. Clean, pure, innocent, and spiritually renewed.

Are Children Morally Accountable?

If you are reading this while young children are playing nearby, you may doubt the "pure and innocent" state of children. None are more self-centered than little children. Particularly during those "terrible twos" when every other word is *mine!* Learning to share is a painful experience for children. And learning to obey parents is absolutely excruciating. When young children are on the prowl, too many cookies disappear from forbidden cookie jars. And the truth suffers terribly when Mother or Father asks about a broken candy dish.

Do young children sometimes lie, cheat, and steal? Of course they do. Are they often selfish and unsharing? Of course they are. Do they always obey their parents? Certainly not!

But that does not make children unholy or impure. Their misconduct would not send them to hell in the event of an early death. Because they lack sufficient moral capacity, they are not morally accountable.

There are some who would suggest that infants, although not accountable, are nevertheless sinful, impure, and unholy because they came into the world burdened with a "sinful nature." However it is logically inconsistent to say that one may be sinful but not held accountable. We are not talking theological theory here. Let's get

143

to the bottom line. Will "sinful, impure, and unholy" infants without baptism suffer eternal adverse consequences if they should die in that condition? If so, then they *are* being held accountable!

We recognize immature moral capacity in our own legal system. That's why the juvenile justice system is completely separate from adult criminal courts. Moral immaturity is the reason that, under common law, there exists a conclusive presumption that a child under the age of seven cannot be guilty of a crime; and that a child between the ages of seven and fourteen is rebuttably presumed to be incapable of criminal guilt.

This does not mean that the child is incapable of doing a wrongful act, such as stealing. It doesn't mean that the child doesn't know what he is doing. It means that the child is of such immature moral capacity that he cannot fully appreciate the moral consequences of what he knows he is doing.

It is universally agreed in all cultures that a child of tender years should not be put in jail for stealing a toy. Enthusiastically spanked, perhaps, but not incarcerated. Childhood is a time for moral instruction, not spiritual condemnation.

Not even the Old Testament disagrees. The rebellious child who was to be put to death under the law of Moses was not the two-year-old throwing a tantrum, or even the ten-year-old who didn't want to wash the dishes. The example given in Deuteronomy was of a son who was "a profligate and a drunkard" (Deuteronomy 21:20). He was hardly one of the "little children" whom Jesus lovingly blessed.

Moses recognized that children of tender years are not morally or spiritually accountable. Moses, of course, was the very one who had told the Israelites about God's "punishing the children for the sin of the fathers to the third and fourth generation." Yet when the fathers had sinned grievously in the wilderness, it was the fathers alone—not the children—who received the punishment for that sin. Moses said,

> Because of you the Lord became angry with me also and said, "You shall not enter [the land of promise], either. But your assistant, Joshua son of Nun, will enter it. Encourage him, because he will lead Israel to inherit it. And the little ones that you said would be taken captive, *your children who do not yet know good from bad*—they will enter the land. I will give it to them and they will take possession of it. But as for you, turn around and set out toward the desert. . ." (Deuteronomy 1:37-40).

This passage shows that the children were not punished for their fathers' sins, and that no sin of any kind is imputed to the very young.

A child may know good from bad at an elementary level very early in his life, but a child is not *held accountable* for knowing good from bad in a spiritual sense until a certain level of maturity is achieved. Exactly when this point is reached will vary with each child. But even this conclusion is irrelevant to the issue of infant baptism because it is an *inherited* sinful nature, not *acquired* sin, that is put forward in support of infant baptism.

Original Sin—Cause for Error

The notion of original sin, however one defines it, runs afoul of the clear biblical teaching that each person stands on his own in the eyes of God, born innocent and pure. Without the doctrine of original sin, the practice of infant baptism loses its major justification.

If original sin is the reason for such a practice, the wedding ceremony of baptism for infants is a spiritual shotgun wedding that need never take place.

Reflections

1. What effect is implied by the phrase "baptismal regeneration"? Does the Bible teach it?

2. What is the most serious problem with infant baptism, theologically speaking?

3. What is "original sin"?

4. What is the difference between inheriting the specific sins of ancestors and each person being born with a sinful nature?

5. What does Ezekiel teach about the sins of a father and his child?

6. What is the difference between "original sin" and suffering the consequences of a parent's sinful actions?

7. What is a prerequisite for moral accountability?

8. What problem does Jesus' own birth present to the idea of "original sin"?

9. What is the intent of the supposed "immaculate conception" of Mary? Is there biblical evidence for it?

10. In what way do little children represent those who enter the Kingdom?

CHAPTER 10

INFANT BAPTISM—AN ARRANGED MARRIAGE?

The doctrine of infant baptism is forced to try to think through the relation between baptism and faith. But when it does, no matter how it twists and turns, it inevitably finishes up in hopeless blind alleys."

Karl Barth

One chapter on the subject of infant baptism ought to be more than enough theology for someone to wade through. But, for many readers, we still haven't covered the waterfront. If you were baptized as an infant, it may have been for a doctrinal reason wholly apart from original sin. In several fellowships, infant baptism is justified on the basis that infants born to believers are "children of the covenant," and, therefore, *entitled* to be baptized as infants.

In this chapter, we want to explore the implications of this particular viewpoint. However, I do not wish to belabor the matter of infant baptism unnecessarily. Therefore, just as in the last chapter, let me suggest that, if infant baptism is not an immediate concern for you, you may wish to turn to the last sections in this chapter, which deals with the possible use of dedications in the place of infant baptisms. As before, however, if you can bear with us through the entire chapter, I believe you will encounter some surprising serendipities along the way.

Children of the Covenant?

In those fellowships practicing infant baptism for "children of the covenant," a parallel is drawn with the covenant of circumcision, which God made with the faithful patriarch Abraham. In that covenant, God promised that through Abraham's family, all people would be blessed. Some believers see the covenant as a spiritual covenant for all time, viable even today. Because Jesus Christ is both the fulfillment of the covenant and its on-going mediator, the seal of the covenant has become Christian baptism instead of circumcision.

Under this view, baptism is administered to children of Christian believers, just as circumcision was administered to the children of Israel. Infant baptism remains a symbol of family solidarity—in Christ—and is a sign of the covenant and a continuation of the promise made to Abraham.

An example of how this covenant promise is used to support infant baptism is in Peter's statement on the day of Pentecost: *"The promise is for you and your children and for all who are far off,* for all whom the Lord our God will call" (Acts 2:39).

Without doubt, the blessing of salvation through Christ, which was obliquely promised to Abraham, is a blessing for all time. And to that extent, the covenant that brought it into effect is an everlasting covenant. But there are at least three problems with interpreting Peter's promise as a basis for covenant-related infant baptism.

First, the promise to which Peter referred was not the promise made to Abraham—at least, not directly.

Rather, his reference was to God's promise that had just been announced to the crowd in Jerusalem: "Repent and be baptized, every one of you, in the name of Jesus Christ for the forgiveness of your sins. *And you will receive the gift of the Holy Spirit."*

The promise at issue, therefore, is not the one made by God to Abraham, but the promise of the Holy Spirit to all baptized believers. Since that promise is predicated upon repentance, it could not be meant for infants, who are unable to repent.

Second, the baptism that brings about the promise to which Peter referred is "for the forgiveness of sins." As we have already seen, infants are not sinful. Because infant baptism for "children of the covenant" is not based on original sin, as are other views of infant baptism, New Testament baptism under this theory makes even less sense.

Third, an invalid assumption is being made about the "children" to whom Peter says the promise applies. Based on the premise that infant baptism is proper, it is assumed that the promise is for believers and their *infant* children. But the word *children* does not necessarily refer to babies. In fact, because of the previously considered problems of faith and repentance, it is the *least* likely meaning of the word.

Peter was not saying, "The promise is for you and your children, *as children."* Peter was saying to the crowd: "If you repent and are baptized for the forgiveness of your sins, God has promised you the Holy Spirit. And that promise is valid for all subsequent generations as well!"

In this same sense, we might hear a politician say defiantly: "We must be vigilant in protecting the rights of liberty and freedom for our children and their children for generations to come!" In looking to future generations, the politician has no intention other than preserving the adult exercise of those rights. It is particularly true of Peter's reference to God's promise that the word *children* does not necessarily mean infants.

Is Infant Baptism a Substitute for Circumcision?

Comparing baptism with circumcision raises a new set of problems with infant baptism. Christian baptism envisions a person's *acting* in response to faith, rather than *being acted upon* through a ritual about which he has no choice and over which he has no control.

We have already seen that, when baptism is compared with circumcision in the New Testament, it is regarded as a circumcision of the heart—a spiritual circumcision that is inappropriate for an infant. Being baptized by his parents does not indicate the infant's own change of heart.

Remember that baptism, unlike circumcision, is an essential element in the dynamic process of one's *conversion*. With the infant, there is neither necessity for, nor possibility of, conversion.

Not the least of the distinctions between baptism and circumcision is that circumcision was for male infants only. Paul tells us that in Christ,

> "There is neither Jew nor Greek, slave nor free, *male nor female*, for you are all one in Christ Jesus. If you belong to Christ, then you are Abraham's seed, and heirs according to the promise" (Galatians 3:28-29).

In recording the conversion of the Samaritans, Luke stresses the important change that took place in Christian baptism: "But when they believed Philip as he preached the good news of the kingdom of God and the name of Jesus Christ, they were baptized, *both men and women*" (Acts 8:12).

This change goes far beyond the formal inclusion of female as well as male. It goes to the very heart of our covenant relationship with Christ, particularly in the wedding ceremony of baptism. Although circumcision was a sign of God's covenant with Abraham—even before the nation of Israel was brought into being and before its national covenant under the law—there is no question but that biblical circumcision was uniquely Jewish.

Although circumcision did not originate under the law of Moses, Jewish parents participated in the ritual as a matter of corporate acceptability before God. The notion of "corporate salvation" partially explains why circumcision of males sufficed for females as well.

An important part of Christ's "superior covenant," as the writer of Hebrews put it, was the elimination of "corporate salvation," whether Abrahamic, Jewish, or Christian. Through Christ, we approach God individually, as male or female, as Jew or Gentile, as rich or poor— *each in his own conscience, each in his own time.*

When parents take a newborn child to the church for baptism, it cannot escape being an act of corporate significance. The child himself has no individual choice regarding that experience. Apart from washing away sins, which the child does not have, the only other purpose for baptism would be as a rite of entrance into the church. It is the very kind of "corporate salvation" that was eliminated by Christ's death!

Closely tied to "corporate salvation" is the idea of "vicarious salvation," which ran throughout the ritual worship under the law. But under Christ, instead of taking sacrifices to a priest who would offer them to God vicariously on our behalf, we *ourselves* have become priests and can offer up our own sacrifices of praise, prayer, and righteous living (1 Peter 2:5, 9). We no longer need the intervention of a third party. Through Christ we have direct access to God. Instead of coming to God vicariously through families by infant baptism, we approach God one by one.

Still another example of how baptism is different from circumcision is found in the sacrificial death of Jesus. Jesus offered himself as a sacrifice for sin because animal sacrifices couldn't do the job. Likewise, baptism replaced circumcision as a mark of the covenant because circumcision couldn't do the job. Circumcision was never intended for Gentiles or for women.

Through circumcision, God's grace was liberally extended to entire families—yet, ironically, it was limited to only one family, Abraham's. Through baptism, God's grace is limited to individuals who respond personally in faith to Jesus Christ. But, by that very means, it is extended to the whole family of man.

God has not grown less gracious with the passage of time. On the contrary, He has opened His loving arms to *all* the children throughout the whole world. He has broken down the wall between Jew and Gentile and offered hope to *every* child who grows up to accept Jesus Christ—not just the children of Jewish parents. Children are not less favored under the New Covenant than they were under the Old. They have the same moral innocence, and now, in addition, the right to seek God for themselves regardless of their parents' religion.

Of course, there are many parallels between baptism and circumcision. Both came by way of commandment. Both are marks of a covenant relationship. And both are symbols of cleansing and purity. But there are important differences as well. Circumcision was unrelated to personal faith, repentance, and confession; baptism is inseparable from them. Circumcision was for males only; baptism is not. And above all, circumcision was not for the forgiveness of sin; baptism is.

Whatever else may be said about the comparison between circumcision and baptism, one thing is certain: while God unequivocally commanded that male descendants of Abraham be circumcised, He has given no command that the children of Christians be baptized. If, in God's eyes, baptism is a carry-over from circumcision, and if both are equally important for the children of believers, is it reasonable to believe that God would have given no specific instructions regarding infant baptism?

Without question, most Jewish Christians in the first century perceived a difference between the purposes of baptism and circumcision. Much to Paul's chagrin, some of these believers continued to practice circumcision even after they had responded to Christ in baptism. They would have been shocked to learn that God fostered family solidarity through the *baptism* of "children of the covenant."

From their perspective, the circumcision of male children perpetuated their heritage and fulfilled their destiny, while baptism was part of a personal process of faith-oriented, life-changing conversion. The lesson they had to learn, as Paul wrote in his letter to the Galatians, was that circumcision was no longer necessary.

For Paul, the concept of covenant relationship by virtue of "family solidarity" was made obsolete along with the act of circumcision that had symbolized it. This planned obsolescence of circumcision and "family solidarity" answers a question sometimes asked by those who support infant baptism: "Suppose the second-century church had changed the rules and restricted baptism to those who were fully aware of what they were doing. Wouldn't there have been a great hue and cry about such an important change?" The answer is that the dramatic change came in the first century, and there *was* a great hue and cry.

In the well-documented controversy between Jewish and Gentile Christians, the front page headlines were all about the continued necessity of circumcision. But among the more fundamental disagreements on page two was the issue of corporate versus personal salvation. As framed, the issue was this: are we saved through a sense of national or family relationship with God, or through individual faith?

Paul's rejection of circumcision led naturally and logically to the rejection of salvation by national or familial solidarity. Personal faith leading to a covenant relationship initiated through baptism was the innovative hall-mark of Christianity. While Jewish Christians did not easily accept that revolutionary idea, it marked a dramatic turning point in man's response to God.

How Did Infant Baptism Begin?

If Christian baptism was done for a purpose different from circumcision, how did the practice of infant baptism ever begin? Some believe that it began when parents of seriously ill children became nervous about the spiritual condition of their children and had them baptized "just in case." This explanation would correspond to the growing fascination with the doctrine of original sin in the early Christian centuries. Yet the practice may have had its roots long before infant baptism became associated with a doctrine of infant jeopardy.

Even without any hard historical evidence, one logically could expect that infant baptism might have been practiced by at least a few early Jewish Christians who might have accepted Paul's teaching only "halfway." By way of compromise, they may have grudgingly conceded a change from circumcision to baptism as a sign of covenant relationship, but retained it for infants who were "children of the covenant." This possibility makes even more sense when you consider that Jews in Jesus' day were already familiar with the baptism of children as part of proselyte baptism. When a Gentile was converted to Judaism, he and his sons would be circumcised, and the entire family—wife, children, and perhaps even servants—would be totally immersed to wash away all Gentile impurity.

In the context of a circumcision covenant, the inclusion of children in the transfer of religious identities would have been altogether reasonable. But when family-initiated religion was replaced by individual spirituality under the teaching of Christ, the efficacy of proselyte baptism for children would have been eliminated along with circumcision.

Undoubtedly, not all Jewish Christians would have appreciated the significance of that transition. Indeed, many Christians still have this difficulty. Thus, for them, the perpetuation of baptism for infants would not be surprising.

In whatever way the practice of baptizing babies began in the Christian era, it was inconsistent with the radical change from corporate identification under Judaism, initiated by circumcision, to personal conversion under the lordship of Jesus Christ, initiated by faith-responsive baptism.

No matter how long-standing the practice, or how supposedly tied it might be to previous covenant considerations, the baptism of infants must stand or fall solely upon its consistency with the meaning, purpose, and example of Christian baptism. Using that test, infant baptism falls far short.

The Problem of an Empty Biblical Record

Supporters of infant baptism are quick to point out that, while the New Testament does not command the baptism of children, neither does it prohibit it. But given the adult prerequisites of faith, repentance, and confession, it would have been superfluous for the Scriptures to have added a specific prohibition. No one who sees a movie advertisement promoting an "adult film" needs to also be told that it is "not for children."

Many people urge that, although we have no direct command to baptize babies, we do have examples of infant baptism. They point to the baptism of the "households" or "families" of Lydia (Acts 16:15), the Philippian jailer (Acts 16:33), and Stephanas (1 Corinthians 1:16). They assume that there must have been young children within those households. Of course, if that speculation is all we have to go on, we are skating on awfully thin theological ice. Were it not for the need to justify infant baptism, would anyone have given such speculation a passing thought?

Scholars agree that the word *household* normally included servants and older members of one's family who lived in the same house. Nothing indicates in these passages that infants were included in the baptism of older members of the household.

We must go with what we know: baptism is the culmination of a conversion process that requires a believing, penitent heart and a willingness to confess to the world that Jesus Christ is Lord (Romans 10:9-10). Whoever might have been included in the term *household* would have been required to go through the same conversion process as all the others, a process in which infants simply could not have participated.

Suggesting that members of a believer's household, whether adult or infant, could come into the kingdom on the coattails of the head of the household introduces a method of vicarious salvation not even hinted at in the New Testament.

In the case of the Philippian jailer and those in his household, they *all* acted in faith in response to what *each of them* had heard: "Then [Paul and Silas] spoke the word of the Lord to him *and to all the others in his house*" (Acts 16:32).

Note the ending to the joyous occasion:

> The jailer brought them into his house and set a meal before them; he was filled with joy because *he had come to believe in God—he and his whole family*" (Acts 16:34). [The initial NIV rendering was: "The jailer brought them into his house and set a meal before them, *and the whole family was filled with joy, because they had come to believe in God.*"]

Those members of the jailer's family who were baptized were old enough to believe the gospel personally and to rejoice in its message of forgiveness and salvation.

Apart from the ambiguous references to the baptisms of whole families, supporters concede that there is no other biblical example of infant baptism. However, it is suggested that such a bare record should be expected during the predominantly missionary era at the church's beginning.

The argument is that covenant baptism could operate only for second-generation Christians—those who were children of the first Christian converts. Yet some sixty to seventy years elapsed between Pentecost and the last of God's revelation, giving more than sufficient time to test that theory. Even during that time, there is no biblical example of infant baptism.

Throughout the New Testament era, baptism always followed preaching. Sinners became Christians in active response to the *Word,* not in passive reception of a religious sacrament called baptism, which was vicariously experienced and which automatically regenerated them. In the biblical accounts, believers responded to a message of grace whereby their sins, of which they were acutely aware, were forgiven through their submission to the lordship of Jesus Christ. This was as true at the end of the first century as it was on the day of Pentecost.

The idea of baptizing "children of the covenant" is for many a comforting theological theory. But it is only a theory. There is neither biblical nor historical support for such a practice.

Some Children More Holy Than Others?

In writing to the Corinthians about marriage and unbelieving spouses, Paul distinguished between "unclean" and "holy" children. Some have offered Paul's reference to "holy children" as support for the concept of "children of the covenant."

> If any brother has a wife who is not a believer and she is willing to live with him, he must not divorce her. And if a woman has a husband who is not a believer and he is willing to live with her, she must not divorce him. For the unbelieving husband has been sanctified through his wife, and the unbelieving wife has been

sanctified through her believing husband. *Otherwise your children would be unclean, but as it is, they are holy* (1 Corinthians 7:12-14).

It is claimed that this passage teaches that children of believing spouses are considered holy in a way that children of unbelievers are not. Therefore, they are beneficiaries of the covenant with Abraham and entitled to baptism without the need for a personal profession of faith. But the context reveals that Paul is not addressing either the issue of infant baptism or covenant relationship. More and more scholars among fellowships practicing infant baptism are, for this reason, specifically renouncing such use of this passage.

Paul is addressing the issue of divorce. "Must, or should, the new Christian divorce a spouse who does not believe?" Paul's response is no. Marriage itself is ordained by God—whether one, both, or neither of the parties is a Christian. Without a marriage, Paul says, it is as if the children had been born out of wedlock, "unclean." When the marriage remains intact, the children belong to legitimate parents and are, therefore, "holy."

Understanding this passage any other way raises many thorny issues. For example, whatever privileges might attach to the *children* of such a marriage would necessarily attach to the unbelieving *spouse* as well, for Paul says that spouses are also sanctified by the marriage. If the children are to be baptized because they have been given God's grace, then the unbelieving spouse should also be baptized—and presumably without any choice in the matter! That obviously wouldn't work.

It is curious that this passage should be used to support the idea of "children of the covenant," because in the marriage that Paul addresses, only one of the parents is a believer. There is no reason here to urge "family solidarity" as the basis for special privilege. Furthermore, this interesting situation raises at least one question directly, and a multitude of others that follow on its heels.

Must *both* of the parents be believers in order for the privileges of the covenant relationship to vest? How are we to define "believers"? Need they be only nominal members in a given fellowship, or must the parents be active, committed Christians? If they must be actively involved in their Christian walk, who is to make the judgment as to which couples qualify? If they need be only nominal members of the church, can much be said for the so-called "covenant relationship" through which the children are to be beneficiaries?

If the unbelieving spouse objects to the child's baptism, does that preclude the child's covenant privilege? And what if the parents become Christians shortly after their child is born? Must they anxiously wait for their child to reach an age sufficient to make his own decision? Or does the privilege of the covenant vest at the time the father and mother become Christians?

Even if all the practical complexities could be sorted out properly, the fact remains that, when one's spiritual condition is in any way dependent on the actions or spiritual state of someone else, we are left with a nebulous, unscriptural doctrine of vicarious salvation—dangerous territory indeed when salvation is at stake.

If some of the Jewish Christians wanted to believe in vicarious salvation as "children of the covenant" with Abraham, Paul would have no part of it:

> Nor because they are his descendants are they all Abraham's children. . . . In other words, *it is not the natural children who are God's children,* but it is the children of the promise who are regarded as Abraham's offspring (Romans 9:7, 8).

Paul is telling us that family ties have absolutely nothing to do with salvation. One becomes a child of the promise through personal decision, not physical birth. One becomes a "child of the covenant" by entering voluntarily into covenant relationship with Christ through the wedding ceremony of baptism, on the date of his or her own choosing.

Confirmation—A Substitute Ceremony

In almost every fellowship that practices infant baptism, the supposed efficacy of the act is betrayed by the ceremony known as "confirmation." Few would disagree that confirmation has its origin from church tradition, without any directly identifiable New Testament precedent. But most of those who practice the ritual believe that confirmation is necessary in order to give the person baptized as an infant the opportunity to ratify that passive act through a personal confession of faith.

Others believe that the *ceremony* of confirmation itself is not essential, but insist nevertheless that the *confession* of adult faith is necessary. Relative to the initial efficacy of infant baptism, it is a distinction without a difference.

Under either view, confirmation is the time when "sponsored" juvenile membership in the church becomes personal adult membership. Typically, the young person has been instructed in the church catechism and must be able to recite the accepted creed, and perhaps the Lord's Prayer and the Ten Commandments. Some fellowships, thankfully, require much more than this.

Confirmation is usually a church ritual—often done in groups, perhaps on a "confirmation Sunday." It is quite unlike the spontaneous, individual conversion experiences of early Christian converts. And because confirmation typically falls at a certain stage of adolescence from seven to sixteen years of age, any confession or dedication that takes place as part of the ceremony is subject to serious question.

It is important to stress that the ceremony of confirmation is necessary because of infant baptism. Confirmation was introduced in order to accomplish what baptism itself should accomplish—i.e., a personal decision to be married to Christ. There is no reason to require a personal confession at this point, unless the vicarious confession originally given by sponsors was ineffective. If, in fact, the parents' confession on behalf of the child was doctrinally sufficient at the time the child was baptized, there is no reason to repeat the confession years later.

Deep down, the adherents of infant baptism recognize that, as Karl Barth has suggested, infant baptism is only half a baptism— the last half. And confirmation itself rarely supplies the first half, which is a voluntary, spontaneous, and personal decision to confess one's faith in Jesus Christ as Lord.

Bishop Ussher conceded that point: "As baptism administered to adults is not effectual unless they believe, so we can make no comfortable use of our baptism as infants until we believe." If we can make no comfortable use of infant baptism before personal belief, "sponsored belief" is a (well-intended) charade.

Yale Professor Aidan Kavanagh recognizes the problem with requiring an after-the-fact "confirmation" of what already has been considered to be an accomplished fact:

> If baptism is as irrevocable as we claim it to be and if it is in fact as Bible and liturgy affirm it to be, a passage from death to the life of the risen Lord and his Spirit . . . then we cannot baptize and cross our fingers in the hope that maybe some of those who are baptized will one day become real Christians (*Worship*: Vol. 48, No. 7).

If faith followed remotely by baptism is difficult theology, baptism followed remotely by faith is even more difficult. At least, where there is adult faith before baptism, the delayed baptism is faith-motivated. Nothing in Scripture indicates that faith and repentance ever *followed* baptism.

Even if one supposes that children of New Testament converts were baptized as "children of the covenant," there is no evidence suggesting a two-stage initiation of such children. Nor is there any evidence that they would have been required to experience a confirmation ceremony or in any other way to make a later "adult" confession of faith.

We must passionately avoid the notion that just *any* combination of faith and baptism is consistent with the New Testament pattern of conversion. Where faith follows baptism, no "relation back" theory is possible, for the baptism is not in response to faith. It is not done as an act of submission.

Returning to the analogy with marriage, a combination of infant baptism and confirmation would be like having an arranged marriage at the time of one's birth, with no choice over the selection of one's partner until, at some advanced age, one could decide to ratify the marriage that has existed all along.

Arranged marriages may succeed, but for countless people the "arranged wedding" of infant baptism has been a dismal failure. Fellowships practicing infant baptism may maintain high levels of church membership. However, the evidence is strong that they are not maintaining a high level of faithfulness, commitment, or even attendance.

We are looking at the big picture here. Naturally, there are a number of individual exceptions who have not only nurtured a deep personal faith in Christ, but who have joined Him in His suffering. We cannot begin to count the many believers who have died for their faith, or who have sacrificed secular success to take the gospel to far-flung nations, yet who received only infant baptism.

Unfortunately, the big picture is vastly different. The person whose initiation into a church occurred without any personal input is not likely to be on fire with enthusiasm for a "salvation" he never sought. In neither his baptism as a child nor his later confirmation is there anything that can be equated fairly with a conversion experience.

The problem is aggravated by the ages of those going through confirmation. Although confirmation is intended for *adult* ratification, in actual practice children as young as seven make that important decision. Surely, little spiritual ground is gained with the limited maturity of a pre-teenager.

It must be emphasized once again that confirmation was never a biblical practice for Christians. And consider what that says about infant baptism itself. If confirmation is *essential* to complete one's infant baptism, and if confirmation is not biblical, then infant baptism itself must be foreign to the Scriptures.

Christians Without Communion?

Another important purpose of confirmation is admission to Communion, or the Eucharist, which in most fellowships is refused to infants until confirmation, despite the fact they have been baptized. (Other fellowships celebrate a child's "first Communion" at an early age—for example, seven—and follow that some years later with confirmation.) Considering baptized infants as Christians while refusing them Communion is but another graphic betrayal of infant baptism, resulting as it does in degrees of membership in the church.

This confusion should not be surprising. What else are we to expect when children are given the "mark of the covenant," but not the covenant relationship; the "badge of membership," but not membership itself. The irony is that, with infant baptism, one gets only limited benefits, while covenant benefits in the Old Testament attached automatically and immediately with circumcision.

If infants are excluded from the Communion of the faithful because they cannot fully appreciate its meaning, baptizing infants in the first place is similarly inappropriate. Where age is a prerequisite to full *participation* in the Christian community, it must be a prerequisite to one's *initiation* as a Christian as well.

There is growing dissent among major fellowships refusing Communion to baptized children. Bishops, priests, scholars, and authors, urging consistency of practice, have called for Communion to be offered to all members, whether adult or juvenile. Admirable as consistency is, they are working from the wrong end. In no way can Communion be appropriate for immature children, perhaps still nursing at the breast!

Professor Kavanagh highlights the problem:

> If these priorities [of mature commitment] are to outweigh the desirability of incorporating the children of Christian homes into the full sacramental life of the church, and even to supersede the witness to God's sovereign grace which infant baptism is, then we must abandon infant baptism, not exalt confirmation. And if we are to retain infant baptism, it seems only logical that it should be followed by infant confirmation and communion (*Worship*, Vol. 48, No. 7, p. 394).

The best resolution of the problem, of course, is a return to the biblical pattern of Christian initiation. Instead of looking for consistency in the extension of Communion to baptized children, we should be finding consistency in the denial of both Communion and baptism to infants, who are unable to appreciate the significance of either practice.

Eliminating the Confusion

Communion is not the only problem that crops up when we depart from the biblical pattern. Even a casual glance through the scholarly literature from fellowships practicing infant baptism reveals the many practical questions that arise

For example, at what age should one be confirmed? Is an official confirmation *ceremony* necessary, or can one make his personal profession of faith in some other way? When does the Holy Spirit vest in the individual—at the moment of baptism as an infant, or when one makes his own confession? Is there a place for rebaptism as an adult?

By contrast, when the biblical pattern of adult-believing baptism is followed, none of these questions arise. The conversion process takes place in one integrated dynamic, with baptism being the response that emerges from a newly formed faith. The benefits that attach to one's conversion—initiation into the church, receipt of the Holy Spirit, and Communion—are simultaneous. There are no categories of Christians. No double standards. No headaches for theologians.

Confirmation and Religious Division

Perhaps one of the most unfortunate effects of the practice of confirmation is its contribution to religious division. We are told by some supporters that, while infant baptism makes one a member of Christ's universal church, confirmation is necessary in order to give a person membership (that is, to "fully enfranchise" them) in a particular denomination. One writer has suggested that, because in a fallen world the church has split into various denominations, it is unfortunately necessary "to bed down in one or another of them." And, for him, confirmation makes this "unfortunate necessity" possible!

But if division among the Christian community is the result of a fallen world (and it is), then we ought to do all that is within our power to eliminate such division, even if it means giving up popular practices that perpetuate it. Christian baptism in the New Testament gave Christians full enfranchisement in the only church in which we need to have membership—the universal body of Christ. How long will it take for us to join together in the "one faith" through the "one baptism?"

Difficulties in Every Direction

The doctrine that "children of the covenant" are *entitled* to be baptized as infants presupposes a *need* for such baptism. But, as we have already seen, infants simply do not come into this world in spiritual jeopardy. Saying that an infant is *entitled* to baptism is like saying the children of those who have recovered from the flu by virtue of having taken medicine are also "entitled" to take the same medicine even though they never had the flu in the first place! It makes little sense to say that infants are entitled to baptism when, as sinless children, they don't even need baptism's remedial purpose.

The baptism of infants puts the cart before the horse. There is a washing before one is spiritually unclean; forgiveness before one has sinned; and an acceptance of Christ before one has known Him.

Practically, there is the problem of infants entering into a covenant before possessing the maturity that such covenants require. In secular affairs, we recognize that a juvenile lacks the legal capacity to enter into a contract. Young people under a certain age, usually fourteen to sixteen, cannot be legally married—*even with parental consent*. Does it make sense, then, that one should be able to enter vicariously into the most important commitment he will ever make—a "decision" having eternal consequences—long before the age we would permit him to enter into a contract or into matrimony?

The truth, of course, is that the infant does not make any decision, or confession, or commitment. Saying that the child does those things through the words and actions of "proxies" is liturgical fantasy. Under no circumstances, secular or religious, is the effectiveness of a proxy held in abeyance until subsequent ratification.

If we do not have a *binding* proxy, exercised *at the request of* the one who has the right to decide, then what we have is merely an *expression of hope* for future acquiescence. If hope alone is all we have, then no decision of any consequence has taken place. With regard to salvation, the formality is simply window dressing—no more.

Why is it that when we read the Scriptures we never once find—even by implication—the notion of "infant baptism," "family solidarity," or "sponsors"? When we read the passages relating to circumcision, why is there no function corresponding to that played by "godparents" in infant baptism?

If "family solidarity" is a key Christian concept, why did Christ repeatedly urge people to respond individually, regardless of what their fathers and mothers had done spiritually? And note the implications of "family solidarity" when it is considered in the reverse. For example, if the father *rejects* Christ, can we still feel comfortable with the idea that, when the head of the family acts, he does so for the whole family?

Trapped by Inconsistency

In researching the subject of baptism, I was intrigued by the many logical flip flops writers make in support of infant baptism. Trying to follow this linguistic waffling is like watching a caged animal running wildly back and forth to avoid seeing itself in mirrors that have been placed at both ends of the cage. The further he runs away from one problem, the closer he comes to another. When trouble appears in that direction, he is forced to circle back to his original vulnerable position.

The best illustration of this is found in *Baptism—Its Purpose, Practice and Power,* by the Anglican scholar Michael Green. I wish I had written his first four chapters, which urge eloquently and persuasively the importance and necessity of baptism. "You are not a Christian until you are baptized," Green says boldly! But, in the course of attempting a biblical justification for infant baptism, Green repeatedly wanders in a wilderness of inconsistency.

For example, in support of the practice of confirmation, Green says (with emphases being mine) that, "Somebody baptized as an infant has not had the opportunity for public and personal confession of his commitment to Christ. He needs that. *It is an integral part of Christian initiation.*" Yet only a few pages before, he has said, "Confirmation is not the topping up of baptism as

167

the entry into the Christian life.... It is no supplementary rite.... *Baptism alone is the rite which initiates a person into the church;* not baptism and something else, i.e. confirmation." If baptism alone initiates, then a public and personal confession made years later cannot be an *integral part* of the initiation process.

At another point, Green notes with pride that Anglicans now see baptism as the sole initiatory rite, "in reaction against the theory of *two-stage* initiation which dominated Anglicanism earlier this century." But only pages later he observes: "In baptism *followed by confirmation* you have the fullest possible expression of Christian initiation that liturgy can devise."

In thus joining baptism and confirmation, Green is facing the fact that without the *second* stage (personal commitment and profession of faith) the *first* stage (infant baptism) has no dynamic conversion value. Infant baptism is not the sole and *complete* initiatory rite he would want it to be after all.

One final example. Drawing from Galatians 3:27, Green observes correctly that "baptism means incorporation into Christ." Later, in struggling with the issue of when a baptized infant is "born again," Greene says that, "The Anglican Church certainly does not believe that all baptized children are 'regenerate' in the full sense of 'spiritually reborn.'"

What a remarkable set of conclusions! Are we truly to believe that a person can be incorporated into Christ without being spiritually reborn? Under the old covenant of circumcision, of course, it was indeed possible for one to be incorporated into Israel without having a change of heart—perhaps ever. Not all Israel was Israel! But in Christian baptism, spiritual rebirth and incorporation into Christ go hand in hand.

Michael Green is not alone in having to dance around the issue of personal faith and infant baptism. Every other writer I have read in support of infant baptism has done the same awkward two-step. Once you depart from the New Testament pattern of adult, faith-responsive baptism, there's no way to avoid arguing against oneself.

An Alternative to Infant Baptism

This book resulted from conversations with a number of dear friends, many of whom are from churches that practice infant baptism. They all are God-fearing, God-worshiping, and Christ-centered people whose lives epitomize the Christian walk. For these, infant baptism has not been a barrier to a strong personal faith in Christ.

Despite my deep concern regarding infant baptism, I recognize that the expression of commitment by parents who take seriously their vows of sponsorship in the rite of infant baptism has been the beautiful beginning in the life of many children who have grown up and matured in the nurture and admonition of the Lord. What a great debt all of us owe when we are blessed with loving Christian parents!

Perhaps, then, there is something of value in the idea of infant baptism. If it is biblically wrong for parents vicariously to confess faith for their infant children, it is biblically right for parents to dedicate their own efforts toward instilling a personal faith in those same children. If it is biblically wrong for the church to administer baptism to "children of the covenant," it is biblically right for the church to accept responsibility for helping its children to grow up knowing the covenant relationship Christians have with Christ.

If it is biblically wrong for children to be baptized before they can come to know God's will for their lives, it is biblically right that friends and relatives in Christ recognize their individual and collective responsibility to the newborn to be living examples of God's will.

There are few more poignant passages in all of Scripture than the story of Hannah dedicating her son Samuel to God. Barren for years, Hannah wept often and prayed to the Lord, vowing that, if He would deliver her a son, she would give the child over in service to Him. When her prayer was answered with the birth of Samuel, Hannah kept her promise, took the boy to Eli the priest, and there dedicated Samuel to God:

> "As surely as you live, [Eli] my lord, I am the woman who stood here beside you praying to the Lord. I prayed for this child, and the Lord has granted me what I asked of him. *So now I give him to the Lord. For his whole life he will be given over to the Lord.*" And he worshiped the Lord there (1 Samuel 1:26-28).

In a sense, every mother is barren until God sends the miracle of birth. And in that sense, all parents should share Hannah's attitude of dedication so that, all their lives, their children will be "given over to the Lord."

Although my mother and father raised me up in the "knowledge and fear of the Lord," for which I have always been grateful, only recently my mother revealed her prayer at the time I was born, dedicating me to God's service. Knowing about her prayer has caused me to consider seriously how God may be using my life, and has given me the sense of parental participation that my friends have expressed regarding their baptism as infants.

Perhaps this is a way that we might move closer to the scriptural teaching and example regarding the children of believers. Instead of baptizing them prematurely, why not simply join with the family and with the church in praying God's blessings on them, and on us, as they grow in knowledge, understanding, faith, and spirit. Involving the church through prayer permits the church, as a "family," to share in the new birth. Through that prayer, the church affirms both the responsibility of the parents to raise the child in the Lord and its own share in that responsibility.

A dedication of ourselves to a child's spiritual support is altogether fitting—whether that dedication takes place publicly in a formal ceremony or privately in our prayers to God. Even if such a "dedication" is but a mere shadow of Hannah's literal gift of her son to God's service, we will have taken giant strides toward achieving solidarity among God's spiritual family without resorting to an unbiblical practice.

Unless it is improperly made a formal substitute for infant baptism, the "dedication" of the parents to the task of rearing a newborn child in the faith raises no concern about an artificially initiated covenant relationship. That such a consecration under the old law was distinct from circumcision is seen even at the birth of Jesus our Savior:

> On the eighth day, *when it was time to circumcise him,* he was named Jesus, the name the angel had given him before he had been conceived.
> When the time of their purification according to the Law of Moses had been completed, Joseph and Mary took him to Jerusalem to present him to the Lord (as it is written in the Law of the Lord, *"Every firstborn male is to be consecrated to the Lord"),* and to offer a sacrifice in keeping with what is said in the Law of the Lord: "a pair of doves or two young pigeons" (Luke 2:21-24).

Just as consecration was distinct from circumcision (and not a sign of covenant), prayers of dedication do not substitute for the child's later decision as an adult to become a Christian through penitent faith and baptism.

Consecrating a child to God today need not, of course, be limited either to male children or to the firstborn child. A prayer of dedication is appropriate for every parent and child. If Jesus were among us on earth today, He would still be placing His hands on children and praying for them—all of them. And so should we.

Infant baptism is the right idea, done for all the wrong reasons. Instead of worrying about little children's being condemned to hell, or in some other way being deprived of the eternal presence of God, we should praise God for their refreshing innocence and do everything we can to help them maintain that purity.

Instead of robbing children of a true conversion experience, under the premise that they are "entitled" to baptism, we should lead them to *want* to share in the joys of the covenant relationship we ourselves have with Christ.

Instead of forcing children into an "arranged marriage" with One they have never met, we should bring them to know Christ so intimately that their love for Him will lead naturally and confidently to their own wedding ceremony of baptism and to a life of dedicated service in His holy name.

Reflections

1. What was the nature of the covenant God made with Abraham, and the rite of male circumcision?

2. What are the similarities and differences between that covenant and Peter's promise to believers in Acts 2:38, 39?

3. Does the New Testament teach salvation through family solidarity? Discuss corporate versus individual covenants.

4. Review the history of infant baptism and the reasons why it was instituted.

5. What do we know about the so-called "household baptisms" recorded by Luke?

6. What is the origin and purpose of the rite known as confirmation?

7. What practical problems and inconsistencies are presented by the practice of confirmation?

8. Does it matter if faith precedes baptism or baptism precedes faith?

9. What might the church practice which would achieve the aims of parental dedication without being unbiblical?

10. What responsibility does the congregation have in the spiritual nurturing of its children?

CHAPTER 11

BAPTISM—A SURPRISE VILLAIN

"Men can be attracted but not forced to the faith. You may drive people to baptism, but you won't move them one step further in religion."

Alcuin

All over the world there are millions of people who call themselves "Christians" because, through the joint efforts of their parents and the church, they were "baptized Christian," and are therefore not Jewish, Hindu, Buddhist, or Muslim.

They may never have read the Bible to see what Christ has to say to them; they may never have darkened the doorway of a church since the day they were brought to be baptized; and they may never have given the significance of the Christian walk the slightest passing thought. But question whether they are Christian, and you'll risk greatly offending them.

In fact, if you are in the wrong part of Eastern Europe, they may even shoot you to defend their "Christian" culture and identity. And if you are in Belfast, Northern Ireland, two different kinds of "Christians" will defend

⁺ heir religious heritage with rocks, bottles, and even bombs, if necessary, whether or not they ever take their faith ser ously otherwise.

In Western Europe and Great Britain, virtually all citizens are members of established state churches and therefore think of themselves as "Christians"—despite the fact that the percentage of those who are active believers is embarrassingly low.

Closer to home, thousands of people calling themselves "Christians" because they have been baptized into a "Christian" society are turning to Eastern religions and self-worshiping human-potential belief systems, claiming all the while that they are still "Christians." They haven't a clue that such Eastern teachings as karma and reincarnation are wildly inconsistent with the Christian doctrines of resurrection, Judgment Day, heaven, and hell. Nor does it seem to matter that Jesus is put on a par with Buddha or Krishna. Because they were "baptized Christian," they will always be "Christian," no matter what they believe.

Even within mainline Christian fellowships, church buildings are filled Sunday after Sunday with thousands of worshipers who attend faithfully, yet routinely. When the doors are open, they are there, but only out of habit or family expectations or, perhaps, a sense of guilt. During the week, you won't find them reading the Scriptures to search out God's truth. You won't discover them talking about God with their neighbors. They don't pray personal prayers. They don't visit the sick. Nor could they give more than a superficial explanation of Christian doctrine.

These nominal Christians are regular in church attendance, but have no personal relationship with God. Nevertheless, in their minds they are good Christians, if for no other reason than that they have been *baptized* "Christian" and have never rejected their initiation into the church.

Why Nominal Christianity?

Why has baptism been such an insignificant factor in the lives of so many millions of people throughout the centuries? Why have so many been baptized and yet so few been truly converted? Even more intriguing, why were they baptized at all? If they have chosen it, why has it led to such minimal participation in Christian worship, work, and fellowship?

The immediate answer is that, in fact, most of the world's nominal Christians have never made a personal decision to be baptized. It was their parents' decision to have them baptized. Being baptized as infants was not something *they* had chosen to do; it was something that *others* had chosen to do to them. If, after the fact, millions had figured out what faith and commitment were all about, many more millions had never come to appreciate the significance of their vicarious baptisms.

But infant baptism is not the only culprit. There are also millions of nominal Christians who grew up in fellowships where infant baptism is not practiced. They may have personally chosen to be baptized, but they have never made serious personal commitments as godly believers. Given those circumstances, it would be surprising indeed if these adolescents had a significantly greater foundation for lasting faith than those who were baptized as infants.

Early-Youth Baptism

The issue of spiritual maturity is not a concern solely for those who practice infant baptism. It should be of equal concern in fellowships that reject infant baptism but routinely baptize preteens and early teenagers. Is there really much difference?

We have already noted that young people of that age cannot legally sign a contract. Nor can they enter into a marriage—even with parental consent. Add to that the fact that they cannot vote, defend their country, drink alcoholic beverages, purchase tobacco, or even drive a car, and you are talking about a person too young to make the most important commitment of his or her life. (If someone were to suggest that Jewish boys became "sons of the law" at the age of twelve, we should remember that personal conversion was not a part of their experience. Nor was their bar mitzvah related to the forgiveness of sin and salvation.)

How little confidence we have in God's grace! We are so incredibly fearful of what might happen if a nine-year-old died before being baptized that, all too often, we fill his mind with terrible visions of hell and tug on his emotional strings until he finally succumbs to the pressure and is baptized. Early-youth baptisms are little better than infant baptisms. At least baptized infants are spared the emotional trauma often associated with early-youth baptisms.

"But what if they are never baptized when they get older?" asks a worried parent. Is *that* our concern? If so, we are hedging our bets on a premature expression of commitment in much the same way as infant baptism. If the youngster does not fully appreciate the meaning of baptism, his baptism is as meaningless as is the infant's. A body has been plunged beneath the water, but nothing spiritual has happened. It is form without substance; act without action. Therefore, if early-youth baptism is the only baptism one ever experiences, it likely will have been in vain.

The fear that one will never be baptized at a later age betrays the emptiness of a premature baptism. It says we don't trust a more mature person to decide to be baptized. It confirms that we encourage earlier baptisms because we know we won't have sufficient influence on them when they've reached a point of really thinking for themselves.

The lesson we must learn is that commitment to Christ is a personal decision that must be entered into only when one is fully informed and fully aware. Like infants, most younger adolescents lack the capacity to make so important a personal decision as baptism. Too often, the result is a young person who is baptized, but is never converted. Is *that* what parents really want? Can we gain any comfort in seeing a pre-teenager baptized, only to see him plod on for the rest of his life as a nominal Christian or actually to fall away from the Lord because he never fully appreciated the importance of his commitment?

The statistics regarding adolescent baptisms are clear: early youth baptisms result in high percentages of church dropouts. In a study done by Dr. Flavil R. Yeakley, Jr. *(Why Churches Grow,* Christian Communications, Inc.), only 10% of those who were baptized before the age of twelve remained faithful or were satisfied with their original baptism. Even for those who were baptized at the age of twelve, only 44% remained "faithful church members." Among these, of course, only God knows how many of them truly made strong personal commitments of faith beyond routine church participation.

The Domino Effect

The aftermath of early-youth baptisms should be a concern to more than uneasy parents. Entire fellowships are experiencing spiritual malaise because so many of their members came into the church prematurely. If people are never truly converted, it matters not that they have gone through the motions of baptism—not even a baptism they may personally have chosen.

Given such questionable results with personally chosen early-youth baptism, and drastically more disastrous results with parent-chosen infant baptism, it is little wonder that, for centuries, the church has suffered drastically at the hands of nominal Christianity. For too long, "baptized but unconverted" has been the death knell of the church. Respectable membership rolls have been maintained at the expense of languid participation from within and sluggish church growth from without.

179

Whatever else it may be, baptism ought to be part of a conscious, well-considered conversion experience. Anything less than that permits a person to claim false security in an act that, in Scripture, is tied to informed participation and deep personal commitment. Anything less than that fills the church with those who wear the right label, but who don't appreciate what it means to become a new person in Jesus Christ.

Baptism ought to be the greatest of all sacred rites. Instead, doctrinally-misunderstood and wrongly-administered baptism has quietly and methodically been snuffing out the life of the church.

Some might say that lack of a true conversion, not baptism, is the real villain. They might point, for example, to the many unquestionably-dedicated believers who have never been baptized at all. And certainly the lack of personal conversion is the ultimate villain. But unbiblical baptism is one of the main reasons for that villain's continued existence and, unfortunately, is the more subtle contributor to nominal Christianity.

On the Big Screen

In the larger picture, the millions who have been routinely baptized as infants are of far greater concern than the truly converted who have never submitted to Christ in baptism. While the latter need to respond to Christ in obedient baptism, the odds are that the former have never even been personally converted.

Obviously, not all who have been baptized as infants or as young adolescents have suffered from a lack of faith and good works. Some of the most zealous missionaries and courageous martyrs in the history of Christianity were baptized involuntarily as infants. Who could possibly count the many who have sacrificed their lives for the cause of Christ? Who could ever know how many committed believers have kept the gospel alive long enough for the rest of us to even have the opportunity to discuss the finer points of baptism?

Despite these countless exceptions, however, the vast majority of those baptized as infants have turned out to be only nominal Christians. Most of these were baptized by churches that, at least historically, have administered the rite of baptism indiscriminately and perfunctorily. Because those who have administered infant baptism have been unable or unwilling to distinguish between faithful and unfaithful parents, the general practice throughout the world has too often resembled an assembly line in which anyone who shows up at the church door is entitled to have their child baptized.

From the perspective of the parents, the typical motivation for having the child baptized appears to be a mixture of family tradition, social expectation, and subtle church pressure, including the not-so-subtle notion that unbaptized children who die will go somewhere other than heaven.

The motivation of the church itself is too often suspect when the baptism of infants has the effect of artificially bolstering official membership rolls. In Europe, where state churches are financed by tax money, officially promoted infant baptisms may actually be necessary to insure a stable tax base for those churches.

Even if that financial interest played no role whatever in the churches' practice of baptizing infants, the reality remains that, through the practice of indiscriminate infant baptism, virtually every citizen is an official member of the state church, yet only small minorities in each country grow up to be active, committed believers.

Sometimes it seems that the official church survives only to initiate the newborn into the world, to perform officially sanctioned weddings, and to usher the dead into the world to come. Is it any wonder church membership rolls remain high while active spiritual involvement—or even church attendance—is abysmal?

Vulnerability Through Self-Deception

Unfortunately, the problems associated with infant baptism—and early-youth baptism, for that matter—often hit hardest in the lives of those who may have been raised by godly parents but who have never personally made a mature spiritual commitment. Because they "grew up in the church," they may assume they have a spiritual insurance policy, good for life. When they read in the Bible that baptism is an integral part of the conversion process, they can say with confidence, "No problem there; I've been baptized."

It is all too easy for them to confuse an act of baptism (either vicariously or prematurely participated in) with a knowing, committed faith. Ask many of them "the reason for the hope that lies within" and you are likely to get blank stares. And all too often there is spiritual failure when difficult moral challenges arise.

Personal faith! That is the crying need of the church. A knowing faith! That is what sustains. Baptism is reserved for adults or responsible young people for good reasons. It cannot be overstated that what is at stake is a mature, reflective conversion experience that allows a person to know why he is a Christian and why he has consciously chosen to submit his life to Christ. There are literally millions of people in the world who are Christians in name only. They are "Christians" simply because their parents happened to be "Christians" and had them "baptized" in a "Christian" church.

Bad Doctrine Has Devastating Spin-Offs

Nominal Christianity harms Christian evangelism in at least two significant ways. First, those who are unconverted are likely to have little interest in converting others. And, second, when the unsaved of the world look around at the unconverted lives of so many nominal "Christians," they understandably want no part of such a religion.

Bad doctrine is not just bad doctrine. Bad doctrine puts the whole Christian community into a tailspin.

One might question, "Why spend time writing a book addressed to the Christian community on the subject of baptism when there is a world filled with people who have never professed belief in Jesus Christ?" But it doesn't take much reflection to see what a sad testimony the weakened Christian community has been presenting for centuries to a lost and dying world.

Sometimes the biggest hurdle one faces in presenting Christianity to the unchurched or disbelieving is "Christianity" itself. Nominal Christianity is killing the church! And one of the most significant factors leading to widespread nominal Christianity is routine, traditional infant baptism or early-youth baptism.

Reformation or Elimination?

Fortunately, more and more fellowships are admitting that the administration of infant baptism has been an embarrassing scandal, and serious efforts toward reform are being made on a number of fronts. In the United States in particular, churches practicing infant baptism are now almost uniformly refusing to baptize infants unless there is evidence that the parents will make a conscientious effort to nurture their children spiritually.

But is it possible that we could be fooled about this long overdue housecleaning? Will administrative reform of an unbiblical practice ever eliminate the core of the problem? Does infant baptism need only reformation, or is total elimination in order?

And what about early-youth baptism? Does it, too, need eliminating? When a person voluntarily decides to be baptized, does that necessarily mean he or she has made a well-informed decision? Is early-youth baptism any more biblical than infant baptism? Can its contribution to nominal Christianity be justified?

Who ever would have thought that baptism could be at the heart of the problem behind nominal Christianity? On anyone's list, surely it would be the least likely suspect. But, in both individual lives and in the big picture, what we believe and practice about baptism is vitally important.

For all of us in the Christian community, the simple fact is that we can no longer afford to allow baptism—the ultimate symbol of personal commitment to God—to continue to be misunderstood and abused. We can no longer allow it to be a doorway to nominal Christianity throughout the world. The popular practices of infant baptism and early adolescent baptism must forever be abandoned if we are to see a widespread renewal of personal faith and conscious commitment to the cause of Christ.

That baptism should be the least likely suspect will not excuse our inattention to its potential for villainy. Unbiblical notions of baptism have killed the church for too many generations. Satan is a wily deceiver. If he can bring ruin to the church through its most sacred practice, it surely must give him all the more pleasure. Ours is the generation in which his smug satisfaction should come to an end. Baptism must no longer be Satan's pawn; we must restore it to its rightful position as a monument to personal faith, and to an informed and loving commitment to God.

Reflections

1. In what way has the church been affected by those who are baptized but unconverted?

2. What practical problems and inconsistencies are presented by the practice of early-youth baptisms?

3. What role do parents have in bringing young people to the point of baptism at a proper time?

4. What level of maturity should a child have before being baptized?

5. Is knowing right from wrong enough? Knowing about Christ as Savior? Knowing enough to ask to be baptized?

6. How can parents answer a young child who wants to be baptized before sufficient maturity to do so?

7. What burden has been placed on youth ministers to "get the children baptized?"

8. What is the danger of early-youth baptisms which lack adult-like commitment?

9. How has the practice of early-youth baptism affected the church's evangelistic outreach?

10. How can the church revitalize large numbers of members who may be only nominal Christians?

CHAPTER 12

WHEN THE MARRIAGE FALTERS

"In baptism, the direction is indicated rather than the arrival."

Frederich Rest

"Should I be rebaptized?" That searching question may come from one who was baptized as an infant and is, only now as an adult, seeing the need for a personal conversion experience, including baptism. And for that person, the answer may come rather easily. The question itself reveals an understanding of the need for a personal, faith-responsive act of baptism.

For those baptized as infants, the fact that their parents had them baptized is reason for gratitude—gratitude for the precious gift of such godly parents. But their parents' love and concern does not satisfy their own responsibility to obey Christ's command regarding baptism. Nor does it allow them the first joyful moment of being spiritually renewed through a personal relationship with Christ.

For the adult believer, nothing can take the place of his or her own wedding day with Christ. For such a person, it is the first baptism of choice, and the only baptism that conforms to biblical teaching and example. Strictly speaking, then, it cannot be said that what someone experiences in this adult baptism is a "rebaptism." It is simply New Testament baptism, personally chosen, personally experienced.

The one biblical example of rebaptism (Acts 19) involved twelve men who had acted sincerely and conscientiously in being baptized under John's baptism. Yet, because they had not been baptized into the name of Jesus and had not, therefore, received the Holy Spirit, Paul "rebaptized" them—or baptized them properly for the first time.

If the twelve men who had participated in personally-chosen adult baptism were required to be baptized again, surely a vicariously-experienced infant baptism requires the same response.

Naturally, there has been vigorous opposition to rebaptism by those who practice infant baptism. If, like them, we assumed that infant baptism is a genuine, effective baptism, then indeed rebaptism would be unwarranted. However, it's not true that "a baptism is a baptism," as some contend. If it were, we could hardly get closer to baptismal regeneration—or worse yet, magic.

Would a baptism be a baptism, for example, if all the participants were acting in a play? Would a baptism be a baptism if the participants were acting under threat of coercion? "Of course not," one might quickly point out, "those baptisms weren't *meant* to be baptisms." Yet, for the one most centrally affected by infant baptism—the infant—neither is his baptism. There are, in fact, elements of both play-acting and coercion in infant baptism when parent proxies pretend to speak on behalf of a baby who lacks any free choice about what is going on around him.

What About Adolescent Baptisms?

A more difficult situation arises when one questions the value of his or her adolescent baptism. Upon reflection, one might be concerned that he or she decided to be baptized for the wrong reason. For example, one might have acted out of an inordinate sense of fear, instilled by a hell-fire-and-damnation sermon. Fear is obviously an inappropriate motivation for the wedding ceremony of baptism, in which Christ lovingly asks for our hand in a marriage of two committed spirits.

Or perhaps someone succumbed to parental or peer pressure and had himself dunked in the water just to get everyone off his back. A close friend of mine who was "nudged" into being baptized at the age of eight remembers feeling at the time that there was a world of sin out there to be explored. Faced with a pressured baptism, he mentally reserved the right to explore that enticing world some day! Not surprisingly, during his college days, he decided to be rebaptized. What bride wants to be shoved down the aisle by either family or friends?

Or perhaps your baptism was the result of a group initiation syndrome. Everyone else was doing it and you didn't want to be left out. If so, you may be having second thoughts about the significance of your baptism.

The fact that a person *chose* to be baptized does not necessarily guarantee that the motivation for the choice was satisfactory. In moments of reflection—caused perhaps by a confrontation with spiritual emptiness or by a more academic study of the subject of baptism—many have wondered if they should be rebaptized. There are two ways to respond to such doubts.

First, if one is certain that the reasons for his initial baptism were not scriptural, it is right and proper for him to be rebaptized. As with infant baptism, it is stretching the term to say "rebaptized," since sincere, obedient, committed faith was lacking in the heart and conscience at the moment the body was plunged beneath the water. Without proper intent, the external motions of being put under water constitute a meaningless act in the sight of God. Such a baptism can be compared only with a sham wedding.

Yet there is a second response to one who may have doubts about the validity of his youthful baptism. If there is no specific reason to doubt the acceptability of one's baptism, but only a generalized concern about having made so crucial a decision at a time of relative immaturity, it may be helpful to consider a wedding ceremony. Do you know many young married couples who fully appreciated the nature of their commitment when they excitedly said their wedding vows?

Let's face it, many young people who get married don't even know how to balance a checkbook, much less plan a family budget. Many young people of marriageable age have never held a steady job, or cooked a meal, or changed a baby's diaper. Yet for most young couples it still seems to work out. And after years of marriage, through good times and bad, the vows take on added significance.

The wisdom of the years makes most married couples look back with horror on how little they understood about what would be required of them in the years ahead. But somehow it works and, as we have seen, Christ has a way of saving the best till last.

For those who feel they came to the wedding ceremony of baptism with too much youthful naivete, there is probably no reason to be rebaptized, if one is nevertheless confident that he or she was entering into a serious, faith-motivated relationship with Christ through that baptism. Even those who are converted for the first time as older adults could look back in later years and recognize how simple and naive their faith was at the time they first believed. To that extent, we are all the *children* of God—ever learning, ever growing, ever maturing.

Were There Misguided Motives?

Sometimes one's motives for being baptized can nullify the act. For example, if one were baptized in order to please a fiance, he or she might later be concerned that the wedding ceremony of baptism was simply a "marriage of convenience." Often people are baptized in order to pave the way between two people of different faiths.

Of course, a person can act from more than one motivation. But if one concludes that the primary motivation was to please the intended spouse, and not to be joined to Christ, then a more sincere baptism would be in order. Can we believe that Christ was honored if our wedding ceremony of baptism was only a matter of convenience?

Rebaptism and Unfaithfulness

The question of rebaptism sometimes comes on the heels of great moral guilt or spiritual unfaithfulness. It is not unlike the inner struggle of one who has been unfaithful in marriage. What do I do now? Where do I go from here? How can I right the wrong?

When one realizes that he or she has been unfaithful to Christ and to the vows of commitment made freely in baptism, one sometimes wonders if it shouldn't be done all over again from the very beginning. But a look at the marriage relationship gives us the answer. When one has committed the sin of adultery, there is no scriptural call for automatic divorce. Nor is there a call for remarriage. What Christ expects of us in that situation is not remarriage, but *recommitment* to the marriage.

Considering rebaptism in the face of great sin indicates a misunderstanding of the covenant relationship that we entered through believing baptism. We have already seen that Christ has promised to be faithful, even when we are not. "If we are faithless, *he will remain faithful*, for he cannot disown himself" (2 Timothy 2:13).

The best demonstration of the faithfulness of God is His covenant relationship with the people of Israel—His chosen bride—who proved unfaithful over and over again. The Old Testament is filled with God's scathing rebukes of Israel for her unfaithfulness as a bride. Yet it is also filled with reminders that—out of His great love—God forgave and forgave, time and again.

The extent of both God's disappointment and His willingness to forgive is described graphically by the prophet Hosea, who forgave and restored his own unfaithful wife:

> Rebuke your mother, rebuke her,
> or she is not my wife,
> and I am not her husband.
>
> Let her remove the adulterous look from her face
> and the unfaithfulness from between her breasts....
>
> Therefore I am now going to allure her;
> I will lead her into the desert
> and speak tenderly to her....
>
> *I will show my love to the one I called "Not my loved one."*
>
> I will say to those called "Not my people," "You are my people"; and they will say, "You are my God" (Hosea 2:2, 14, 23).

What more beautiful description could there be of God's faithfulness and forgiveness! As Christians, we have the same assurance of grace and mercy when we follow forbidden paths and lose our way spiritually.

Is this forgiving grace an open invitation to unfaithfulness? Because the husband has said, "I will always forgive you," does that free the wife to be unfaithful? Because the wife has said, "I will never leave you," does that free the husband to run around on her? Paul addresses this issue head on in writing to the Roman Christians:

> What shall we say, then? Shall we go on sinning so that grace may increase? By no means! We died to sin; how can we live in it any longer? *Or don't you know that all of us who were baptized into Christ Jesus were baptized into his death?* We were therefore buried with him through baptism into death in order that, just as Christ was raised from the dead

through the glory of the Father, we too may live a new life (Romans 6:1-4).

> *Therefore do not let sin reign in your mortal body so that you obey its evil desires.* Do not offer the parts of your body to sin, as instruments of wickedness, *but rather offer yourselves to God, as those who have been brought from death to life*; and offer the parts of your body to him as instruments of righteousness. For sin shall not be your master, because you are not under law, but under grace (Romans 6:12-14).

Rather than presumptuously treading on Christ's grace and forgiveness, we should be motivated all the more to remain faithful. He does not demand obedience as a tyrannical husband; rather, He compels us to faithfulness through His unbounded love.

Confession and Prayer—Not Rebaptism

Fully appreciating the grace we have through Christ can actually enhance our sense of shame when, inevitably, we are unfaithful. Do we not, then, need to be rebaptized upon our return? The answer lies in a better understanding of the role Christ plays in the forgiveness of our sins. He is both our High Priest and our sacrifice for sin, offered once for all time:

> Day after day every priest stands and performs his religious duties; again and again he offers the same sacrifices, which can never take away sins. *But when this priest had offered for all time one sacrifice for sins, he sat down at the right hand of God* (Hebrews 10:11, 12)

In His death, Christ offered himself once and for all as a sacrifice for our sins. If in baptism we are united with Christ in the likeness of His death, then through the grace of God we have entered into a covenant relationship, once and for all, in which our sins are forgiven.

That doesn't mean, of course, that we will not sin while in that covenant relationship. What it does mean is that, because we are joined to Christ, our intercessor, we have access to God through prayer, and also His promise of grace to cover our sin:

> Therefore, since we have a great high priest who has gone through the heavens, Jesus the Son of God, let us hold firmly to the faith we profess. For we do not have a high priest who is unable to sympathize with our weaknesses, but we have one who has been tempted in every way, just as we are—yet was without sin. *Let us then approach the throne of grace with confidence, so that we may receive mercy and find grace to help us in our time of need* (Hebrews 4:14-16).

In his epistle, James also calls us to penitent prayer:

> Is any one of you in trouble? He should pray. . . . *Therefore confess your sins to each other and pray for each other so that you may be healed.*
>
> *The prayer of a righteous man is powerful and effective*
> (James 5:13,16).

Rebaptism is neither necessary nor appropriate for the sinning Christian who is already in covenant relationship with Christ—no matter how great the sin! As children of God through faith in Christ Jesus, we have access to the Father of mercy through the avenue of prayer.

And this is true even when we feel so terrible about our sinfulness that we can hardly move our lips to utter a prayer. The good news of life in Christ is that, in the wedding ceremony of baptism, we "marry into the family"—Father, Son, and Holy Spirit.

> In the same way, the Spirit helps us in our weakness. *We do not know what we ought to pray for, but the Spirit himself intercedes for us with groans that words cannot express.* And he who searches our hearts knows the mind of the Spirit, because the Spirit intercedes for the saints in accordance with God's will (Romans 8:26, 27).

When a marriage runs into trouble and love hits the skids, husbands and wives are not always quick to forgive or to work toward a healing of the wounds. In human relations, even confessions and apologies do not guarantee healing.

But when our commitment to Christ wavers because of our spiritual complacency, our flirtation with the world, or our unfaithfulness in the Christian walk, John tells us we can know with assurance that our confessions are not in vain. "If we confess our sins, he is faithful and just and will forgive us our sins and purify us from all unrighteousness" (1 John 1:9).

Have you abandoned your first love? Do you feel estranged from Christ and guilt ridden by unfaithfulness? Are you so overwhelmed by sin that the gap between you and God seems incapable of being bridged? If so, prayer from a penitent heart is in order, not rebaptism.

When Paul addressed the Corinthian Christians who had fallen into the sin of religious division, he did not tell them to be rebaptized. But he did *remind* them of their baptisms in which they had committed their spiritual lives to Christ and thereby entered into a relationship of unity with God and with each other (1 Corinthians 1:13). In the same way, our baptism calls us back to God as a visible reminder of the vows we made, and of God's own commitment of faithfulness to us.

Nicodemus was right. Like physical birth, true baptism cannot be repeated. In baptism, we have already come into contact with the only sacrifice that can cleanse us of our sin. Would we wish for Christ to be recrucified?

To think that we can repeat baptism places us in the driver's seat of salvation—as if we could do a better job of it the second time around. Baptism shows that it is God *alone* who saves, through the death of Jesus Christ. Were it otherwise, we would need to be rebaptized at the close of every day, and even that would fall miserably short of justification.

Like the sinful woman who anointed Jesus and wet His feet with her tears, we should love much, for we have been forgiven much. And when sin causes our marriage with Christ to falter, we should rest confidently in our baptism. Penitent prayer, not rebaptism, is how we turn back to God.

Let us look back in wonder and thanksgiving at the wedding ceremony of baptism, through which we have been graciously washed and mercifully cleansed. And let us thank God that He continues to bless us with His promised forgiveness. Praise God for His everlasting mercy!

Reflections

1. What reason is there for "rebaptism" when one's only baptism was as an infant?

2. What reasons might there be for rebaptism when one's baptism was as an adolescent?

3. Under what other circumstances should one be rebaptized?

4. What scriptural example do we have of rebaptism?

5. Does recognition of spiritual immaturity at any age necessarily suggest a need for rebaptism?

6. Should an unfaithful Christian ever be rebaptized?

7. What does God require of the penitent Christian in the face of sin?

8. What statement is being made theologically when one is rebaptized under circumstances which do not suggest the need for a second baptism?

9. How is forgiveness in a marital relationship perhaps different from God's forgiveness when we are unfaithful to Him?

10. What is the significance of your baptism at moments when you acknowledge your sins before God?

CHAPTER 13

SUPPOSE THERE IS NO CEREMONY

"We find Christian baptism closely connected with the death and resurrection of Christ as a solemn rite in which the individual becomes so united with Christ that he dies to sin and rises with a new life

Donald M. Baillie

Are you perhaps disturbed at this point in our study? Are you concerned that a biblical view of baptism excludes most doctrinal approaches to baptism currently accepted within the Christian community? Did your own baptism differ in some way from the biblical pattern? Or are you, perhaps, one of those who have never experienced baptism in any form?

With the greatest reluctance, we must finally address the obvious questions that follow from this study. If adult believing immersion for the forgiveness of sins is the scriptural pattern for baptism, what is the spiritual destiny of the millions of believers whose baptism followed a different pattern?

Do faithful believers who were baptized only as infants stand in eternal jeopardy? Are those who have committed their lives in faithful service to Jesus Christ, but who have never been taught the need for water baptism, spiritually lost? Can it be that those who see baptism as a matter of obedience, but not of salvation, are risking God's judgment?

The thought of condemning to hell the vast majority of believers throughout the Christian centuries is one of the most compelling reasons for the recent moratorium on any serious discussion of baptism. For if any clear conclusions are drawn—beyond a weak "each in his own heart, each in his own way" —then we are inexorably drawn into this judgmental abyss.

It's in God's Hands—Fortunately!

Is it not enough to leave the judgment to God? After all, it is God "who will judge the living and the dead" (2 Timothy 4:1). I, for one, want no part of that responsibility, and even cringe at what Paul suggests when he asks: "Do you not know that the saints will judge the world?" (1 Corinthians 6:2).

But, unfortunately, sidestepping ultimate responsibility for eternal judgment does not end the matter. For each of us must anticipate as best we can what God expects in our lives on earth. Not only do we have important personal decisions to make in that regard, but Jesus has also called us to be teachers—evangelists of both the good news itself and of the spiritual consequences awaiting those who fail to do God's will.

Taken to its extreme, one could place so much emphasis on God's ultimate responsibility for judgment that no Christian teaching would ever be possible. If our answer to every spiritual question is: "Decide for yourself, for only God can judge," then we are useless as evangelists for Christ. On the other hand, if we pontificate about which actions will or will not receive God's ultimate approval, we assume presumptuously the role that only God can fill. A tough dilemma, indeed.

Speaking as one trained in the law, I wonder if we don't need to make a more careful distinction between our best understanding of what the law says, and our speculation about what the judge might decide. Justice is, after all, quite a, separate matter from mere compliance with the law. Justice takes into consideration all of the factors surrounding the failure to obey.

On the other hand, we should be slow to predict the decisions of a Judge who is notoriously merciful and to blithely assume that He always disregards the law in favor of leniency. On more than one occasion, that same Judge has issued harsh words from His seat of judgment.

Our role as believers is to study God's revealed will for our own lives and to share with others our best understanding of what God wants us to do—aware always that our understanding may be wrong. That attitude is a long, long way from making eternal judgments about anyone's spiritual destiny. We must be sure to leave that judgment to the Great Judge.

None of us can presume to know about the eternal destiny of *anyone,* on the basis of *any* question of doctrine—be it predestination, charismatic gifts, the washing of feet, or even baptism. All we can do is give our best efforts to knowing God's will, as revealed in His written Word.

A Question of Obedience

With that understood, there are tough questions to ask. For example, if a person can be saved without baptism simply because he has never been taught the need for it, does it follow that a person who has never been taught about Jesus Christ can be saved without believing in Him? Or more to the point, is ignorance of the law an excuse before God?

Does one's educational level make a difference? Is ignorance an excuse for the illiterate person who can't read and must therefore rely on others, but not for the educated believer who fails to dust off his Bible and search out God's truth? If there *is* a difference, how many of us qualify as illiterate?

Obviously, if you are reading *this* book and have prayerfully considered the issues regarding baptism that it has raised, you fall into neither of these categories. We have boxed ourselves into having to make *some* decision, even if it is a decision to maintain a status quo. If there were ever an "out" based on ignorance of the issues, we no longer have that defense. Each of us must face the question of baptism squarely.

Instead of asking whose understanding of baptism is right, we ought to ask whether we are willing to do whatever God asks, even if we don't fully understand His reason for asking. More important than an understanding of spiritual principles is an attitude of humble obedience.

Pressure to Conform

It is sometimes more difficult to change a doctrinal understanding of what God requires of us than to deal with moral weaknesses that plague us. At least when we struggle with moral temptations, we usually have the support of our families and the church. However, when confronting a different view of Christian doctrine, we often invite the anger of the very ones who ought to support us the most in our spiritual growth. Sadly, a change in belief can be far more threatening to those we love than a change in how we live our lives.

A changed belief seems to condemn others who have not thought about the matter as much as we have or who have considered it, but have not changed their belief. And to be honest, there *is* a sense of condemnation. By seeing a need to be baptized, or perhaps "rebaptized," for example, one makes a statement about the importance of baptism.

And if others are unwilling to consider the need for baptism in their own lives, a kind of unstated defensiveness often arises, as if to say: "Why did you have to go and do that? Now I must either seriously consider it myself or risk your feeling that I don't care about something that is spiritually important."

Or it may be a matter of abandoning tradition and causing the discomfort that inevitably follows. When one challenges a theological position, the typical reaction is: "But we've always done it this way." Or the silent undercurrent from a family may be: "If it was good enough for your mother and your dad, it's good enough for you." Oh, the many subtle ways our peers apply pressure for us to conform!

The wedding analogy suggests a parallel in the agonizing decision one sometimes must make—whether to marry and, in so doing, lose the goodwill of a family who is dead set against the marriage.

Jesus had something to say about that choice, but it can be a hard calling:

> Do not suppose that I have come to bring peace to the earth. I did not come to bring peace, but a sword. For I have come to turn
> "a man against his father,
> a daughter against her mother,
> a daughter-in-law against her mother-in-law—
> a man's enemies will be the members of his own household."
>
> Anyone who loves his father or mother more than me is not worthy of me; anyone who loves his son or daughter more than me is not worthy of me (Matthew 10:34-37).

Obedience often carries with it an enormous price, as Jesus himself discovered. But for those whose baptism places them at odds with their own family, Jesus gives this great promise:

> And everyone who has left houses or brothers or sisters or father or mother or children or fields for my

sake will receive a hundred times as much and will inherit eternal life (Matthew 19:29).

Whether it be family ties, social pressure, or even personal pride, all must be sacrificed in our total obedience to God. The wedding ceremony of baptism is certainly a responsive act of love. But it is also a courageous act of humble obedience—a step we each must take.

The Flock Is Being Led Astray

Having grown up in a Christian fellowship that honored (but incompletely explained) baptism, it is too easy for me to say that everyone else from other fellowships within the Christian community ought to find the nearest pool of water and jump in, in the name of the Father, the Son, and the Holy Spirit. Yet I do wonder how so many Bible-exalting, Bible-reading, sincere believers can fail to see the significance of Christian baptism, and how Christian scholars can attempt to justify infant baptism.

Based on what I have read from the theologians and the clergy, I'm worried less about how God may judge those who haven't been baptized than I am about the disregard of Scripture that permits such shallow thinking about baptism. Little has changed since the days of Hosea, who warned: "My people are destroyed from lack of knowledge" (Hosea 4:6).

The responsibility for the biblical illiteracy that has become epidemic in our own time falls squarely into the lap of those who have been given responsibility for spiritual leadership. Theologians, priests, and clergy take note. Greek and Hebrew scholars, beware. Christian authors, pay attention. Through the powerful words from Ezekiel, God has rebuked us all for leading the people astray:

> Woe to the shepherds of Israel who only take care of themselves! Should not shepherds take care of the flock? . . . You have not strengthened the weak or healed the sick or bound up the injured. You have not brought back the strays or searched for the lost. You

have ruled them harshly and brutally. *So they were scattered because there was no shepherd, and when they were scattered they became food for all the wild animals* (Ezekiel 34:2, 4, 5).

If millions of sincere believers have never come to understand the true significance of baptism, much of the responsibility must go to the spiritual leaders who guide the Christian community. By doggedly following our humanly-derived creeds and traditions, we have scattered God's people in every direction on the subject of baptism. And they have become prey for every enticing theory that comes along to take them away.

I believe there is a great judgment to be faced on the issue of baptism. But it might lead to some surprising results. The end of Ezekiel's vision of the scattered sheep speaks of God's bringing back a remnant of Israel and of a new relationship that would come through the Messiah. Yet its symbolism is also a possible source of hope for those who for centuries have been taught incorrectly about baptism:

> For this is what the Sovereign Lord says: I myself will search for my sheep and look after them. . . . . I will rescue them from all the places where they were scattered on a day of clouds and darkness. . . . I will search for the lost and bring back the strays. I will bind up the injured and strengthen the weak. . . . I will shepherd the flock with justice (Ezekiel 34:11-16).

Where spiritual leaders have failed the Christian community, God may step in to look after the ones who have been led astray. Certainly God does not relieve us of responsibility for our own spiritual misunderstanding or for our failure to comply with what we know God has asked. But Ezekiel's message suggests that God may look with tenderness and kindness on the humble believer who seeks to do His will but is led into spiritual error by those who ought to know better.

Why Make Judgment Necessary?

Are unbaptized believers destined to hell? Are those who have received only infant baptism in eternal jeopardy? Only God knows. On one level, these are questions we have no right even to ask. As seen in this study, there is an abundance of scriptural language that, on its face, regards baptism as an essential part of our turning to God. Nevertheless, I would hope that God might apply the "common law marriage" approach for those who have lived a lifetime of service in His name without having participated in the wedding ceremony of baptism.

We do know that God has promised to shepherd the flock with justice. And as a self-righteous Jonah discovered to his dismay, God is "a gracious and compassionate God, slow to anger and abounding in love, a God who relents from sending calamity" (Jonah 4:2). Nevertheless, in what specific Scripture can we find a promise of leniency on the issue of baptism?

Given a choice, most people would rather have a confirmed reservation than risk flying standby. Why do we feel differently about salvation? It's wonderful knowing we have a merciful God judging us. But why should we put His mercy to the test when we can just as easily do as He commands us? Love doesn't ask what it can get away with. Love asks, "How much can I do to please?"

The wedding ceremony of baptism is such a simple act of obedience, such a rewarding step of faith, and such a lovely way in which to identify with Christ, that anyone who passes it by will have missed one of the richest spiritual experiences God has offered us. Judgment and condemnation should not be the issue. Baptism is about responsive love and joyful celebration.

Reflections

1. Who alone is the Judge of the universe, and who will judge the living and the dead?

2. Is salvation a matter of human obedience or a matter of God's grace?

3. What is our role in teaching others what Scripture has to say about baptism?

4. What should be our attitude regarding those who have faith in Christ but have not been scripturally baptized?

5. In terms of God's final judgment, how should we view our own baptism?

6. What kinds of pressures might keep one from changing his view of baptism?

7. Is it possible that your own view of baptism is affected by those same pressures?

8. Who probably bears the greatest responsibility for doctrinal error regarding baptism?

9. How would you feel if God saved people whose understanding of baptism is different from your own?

10. Does the possibility that Gods' grace may surprise us in Judgment lessen in any way our responsibility to teach what the Bible has to say about baptism?

CHAPTER 14

REASON FOR CONCERN

> *"The Church is the only institution in the world that has lower entrance requirements than those for getting on a bus."*
>
> William Laroe

A friend of mine recently asked me: "Does it really make a difference whether one is baptized? *Really?*" Coming from him, the question was more intriguing than it might otherwise have been, because he believes virtually the same as I do—that baptism is indeed a crucial part of the conversion experience; that it does, in fact, matter; that it was, after all, commanded by Christ. So I knew he believed it made a difference. But I also knew this was not the point of his question. It went far deeper than that.

What he was asking me, and himself as well, is whether *practically* speaking—really and truly—the way in which one might have encountered baptism affects one's Christian walk. Is it possible to sort out Christian teaching and practice on the subject of baptism, only to overlook how individual lives might actually be affected?

It's one thing to believe in something academically or theologically. It's another thing altogether to know deep down in your heart that it really makes a difference.

Honest reflection forces one to look closely at those who have been baptized in the manner of New Testament believers. If theologically they are right in saying that it is only through faith-responsive baptism that we can receive the promised gift of the Holy Spirit, why are they sometimes the ones most likely to downplay the work of the Holy Spirit in their lives? Conversely, why are fellowships that virtually spiritualize water baptism out of existence often the very ones most likely to claim the power of the Spirit?

Why do I look around among those I know and see so many who have been baptized by the "right formula" living lives that exhibit little evidence of spiritual insight and commitment? Conversely, why do I see other friends who were baptized as infants, or not baptized at all, living godly, spiritual lives? If a correct understanding of baptism is so important in theory, why does it appear to be so inconsequential in practice?

Of course, the same questions could be asked about marriage. Why is it that some couples living together without the benefit of marriage have, from all outward appearances, a happy, loving, and even committed relationship? And why is it that so many other couples— married couples—enjoy none of those things? Obviously, a wedding doesn't necessarily guarantee marital bliss! And yet would anyone urge that, for that reason, marriage is not really so important after all?

The fact that there is but "one baptism" does not necessarily mean that each one who is baptized will experience its power in the same way. Some will see it more as a symbol of the relationship with Christ that they have already experienced for many years. Others will see it as the watershed in a changed life—a moment in time in which their entire outlook and actions were dramatically transformed and realigned.

There are some for whom the act of submitting to baptism means everything. Norman Levison, a converted Jew, was such a person. Of his baptism he wrote,

> At this distance of time it is possible for some to argue that baptism is not necessary to becoming a Christian. That may all be very well for the good people of the Society of Friends and others not as good, but for the Hebrew Christian it is a very important matter, for he is cast out from his own people when he confesses his faith in Christ, and thus he needs to have assurance that he is incorporated into the New Israel, for that is in part what Christianity means to him. His reception by baptism into the Church, the Body of Christ, gives him a sense of continuity with the past, and the new relationship to God through the New Covenant realized and ratified in the New Covenant made in his broken body and shed blood ("The Proselyte in Biblical and Early PostBiblical Times," S.J.T., vol. 10, p. 52).

In answer to my friend's question, Norman Levison would answer with trembling voice that baptism is, indeed, *really* important. In his life, it made a very practical difference. And his affirmation could be multiplied many times over by people for whom baptism was a crucial factor in the success of their spiritual commitment to Christ.

A Global Perspective

Looking to individual responses—whether positively or negatively—is the wrong focus. In law, we have an expression that says, "Hard cases make bad law." That is, if the law were shaped only in light of exceptional and often difficult cases, then the law would rarely be beneficial for the whole of society. For example, we don't change the speed limit to 80 M.P.H. just because someone might need to drive that fast in an emergency. Difficult cases should be dealt with on a case-by-case basis, as exceptions to be appreciated uniquely in the pursuit of justice, rather than making them patterns for the norm.

Applied to baptism, this principle calls for us to look beyond individual believers—and beyond given fellowships—to see the larger picture. Being able to look at the big picture is a difficult task for any of us, whether it be a matter of law, economics, or Christian doctrine. Hard cases, involving identifiable people and immediately identifiable problems, grab our attention and concern, whereas the global picture (which involves even greater numbers of identifiable people, if only we could identify them) seems to fade into a theoretical black hole.

To get a handle on this, look for just a moment at the global picture of marriage. Even if it is given that many married couples are miserable and many unmarried couples are happy, would it be better if there were no marriage at all?

If there were no institution of committed love and faithfulness whatever, would the absence of marriage actually change how people live and act? Or as my friend might put it, would it *really* make a difference? Is it just our inability to overcome tradition and upbringing when we answer with a resounding "Yes! It would indeed make a difference"?

The importance of marriage can be seen most clearly in those cases where marriages have failed. Need one point to the correlation between broken homes and the whole spectrum of social problems, from crime to lower educational achievement to a host of spin-off psychological impairments? When marriages are unstable, all of society suffers. And were there no marriage at all, surely the end result would be equally disastrous. If families are the glue that holds society together, it is marriage that holds the family together. Marriage in the big picture makes an unquestionably important, and *very real*, difference.

If we put aside Christ's teaching for a moment and try to see baptism in this global perspective, it is not always easy to see what practical difference baptism would make if all conversion experiences were true, sincere, well-understood conversion experiences, but without a burial in water. But what we have discovered about the nature of baptism strongly suggests that baptism is a tangible anchor for one's commitment to Christ, somewhat like the wedding ceremony is for a marriage.

In the tough times, when we struggle in our Christian walk, there is a visible, identifiable act of commitment to look back on, to steady us. It's the same with virtually any act of initiation. Having an identifiable date and place to remember, and a special act on our part to cherish, has a way of solidifying and making permanent the inner commitment we have made. In faith-responsive baptism, God has blessed us with an anchor of remembrance.

Unity Through the One Baptism

There is yet another way in which our view of baptism makes a real difference- -this time to the body of believers itself. Baptism is not only a very personal trysting place between God and man, but it is also the beginning of our new relationship with other baptized believers.

From the pen of the apostle Paul, we have already seen that our unity with fellow Christians comes through the working of the Holy Spirit, but is clearly tied to our common baptism. *"For we were all baptized by one Spirit into one body*—whether Jews or Greeks, slave or free—*and we were all given the one Spirit to drink"* (1 Corinthians 12:13).

What a call to unity Christian baptism is! That our different baptisms have so tragically divided us, instead of unifying us, suggests that we have not all been drinking of the same spiritual drink. Could it be that the variant forms and misunderstood purposes of our many baptisms have stood in the way of our receiving the precious, unifying blessings of the Holy Spirit?

The unity of the people of Israel was somehow linked to their common baptism into Moses and to the spiritual water which they drank from a source Paul later identified as being Christ:

> For I do not want you to be ignorant of the fact, brothers, that our forefathers were all under the cloud and that they all passed through the sea. They were all baptized into Moses in the cloud and in the sea. They all ate the same spiritual food and drank the same spiritual drink; for they drank from the spiritual rock that accompanied them, and that rock was Christ (1 Corinthians 10:1-4).

Do we today risk disunity in failing to confront the issues of baptism—what it means, its purpose, its proper mode, and its timing in the conversion experience? In our rush to reach beyond the teaching of elementary Christian doctrines, have we simply ignored baptism?

While encouraging us to dig more deeply into our spiritual understanding, the writer of Hebrews surely did not suggest that we can afford to ignore the basics. In fact, he reiterates for us those six basic teachings, without which there is an inadequate foundation for greater spiritual maturity:

> Therefore let us leave the elementary teachings about Christ and go on to maturity, not laying again the foundation of repentance from acts that lead to death, and of faith in God, instruction about baptisms, the laying on of hands, the resurrection of the dead, and eternal judgment (Hebrews 6:1, 2).

We can ill afford to ignore what Scripture has to say to us about baptism—whether it be the baptism of the Holy Spirit, the baptism of suffering, or the believer's baptism in water. All of these baptisms are fundamental to our understanding of the Christian walk.

If we have not ignored the matter of baptism, have we on the other hand accepted without question what denominational creeds have to say about baptism? Or have we clung tenaciously to tradition? And if we have questioned the meaning of baptism among ourselves, have we argued and fussed about the matter with such acrimony that our debates themselves have been contrary to the very spirit of love and peace that baptism is supposed to bring?

The unity of the faith and the unity of God's people are at issue here. It is important for us to see how the "one baptism" fits into the context of that unity. Paul's words to the Ephesians are instructive on this point:

> As a prisoner for the Lord, then, I urge you to live a life worthy of the calling you have received. Be completely humble and gentle; be patient, bearing with one another in love. *Make every effort to keep the unity of the Spirit through the bond of peace.* There is one body and one Spirit—just as you were called to one hope when you were called—one Lord, one faith, *one baptism;* one God and Father of all, who is over all and through all and in all (Ephesians 4:1-6).

While we must surely "contend for the faith that was once for all entrusted to the saints" (Jude 3), we must not be contentious. Trying to understand the true spirit of baptism simply must not lead us to civil war within the Christian community.

The Challenge of Christian Baptism

The challenge to all of us in the Christian community is to rethink what we have understood about baptism. Every fellowship could profit from self-scrutiny. Indeed, some fellowships have already begun that process, quietly and without fanfare.

You might be surprised to learn, for example, that The Order of Christian Initiation of Adults, approved by the Roman Catholic Church in 1972, radically altered that church's centuries-old view of Christian initiation so that now the initiation of adults is to be the *normal* practice. For a church that baptizes roughly eleven infants for every one adult, the idea of actively evangelizing and baptizing adult believers is revolutionary.

Of course, as Professor Kavanagh suggests, "it will literally require an act of God to make it possible for our people to swallow such a radical change." Nevertheless, it is significant that so entrenched an ecclesiastical body as the Roman Catholic Church has been willing to reassess its tradition and to acknowledge a stronger connection between personal professed faith and the act of baptism.

Thank God that at long last, among both Catholics and Protestants, evangelism by procreation is finally being repudiated! And who knows? If we could come closer to a unified understanding of the "one baptism," perhaps we could make giant inroads toward a common understanding of the "one faith"! Even if that greater unity were never achieved, at least baptism will not have been ignored by default.

For each of us individually, there is a challenge to join our Lord and Savior, Jesus Christ, in the likeness of His death, burial, and resurrection through faith and baptism, and then to walk joyously hand in hand with Him in the likeness of His righteous life.

The issue must never be reduced to a question of, "Do I really *have* to be baptized?" The only question is this: "If Christ has chosen me as His own, and if through His divine love and merciful grace He bids me to join Him in the wedding ceremony of baptism—how can I refuse?" Why would I *want* to refuse?

Reflections

1. What conclusions should one draw from the fact that unbaptized believers can have strong faith and deep commitment, while those who are baptized scripturally may live personal lives unworthy of the gospel?

2. If there is "but one baptism," does it have the same meaning to all who experience it?

3. In whose lives may baptism have perhaps more dramatic meaning than in others?

4. How might the Christian community be different if there were no infant baptism? No early-youth baptism? No adult baptism by immersion? No baptism at all?

5. What would the Christian community be like if baptism were universally practiced the same way?

6. Is uniformity of practice more important than biblical correctness?

7. When was the last time your church, fellowship, or local congregation re-examined the Scriptures to determine if its practice of baptism is biblical?

8. What conclusion might be drawn from the fact that a growing number of independent community churches are emphasizing adult believer's baptism?

9. What is wrong with the question: "Do I really have to be baptized?"

10. How has this study been helpful to you in understanding biblical baptism?